SUBSTANCE ABUSE ASSESSMENT, INTERVENTIONS AND TREATMENT

SUBSTANCE ABUSE

INFLUENCES, TREATMENT OPTIONS AND HEALTH EFFECTS

Substance Abuse Assessment, Interventions and Treatment

Additional books in this series can be found on Nova's website under the Series tab.

Additional e-books in this series can be found on Nova's website under the e-books tab.

SUBSTANCE ABUSE ASSESSMENT, INTERVENTIONS AND TREATMENT

SUBSTANCE ABUSE

INFLUENCES, TREATMENT OPTIONS AND HEALTH EFFECTS

TANYA REID
EDITOR

nova publishers
New York

Library of Congress Cataloging-in-Publication Data

Names: Reid, Tanya, editor.
Title: Substance abuse : influences, treatment options and health effects / editor, Tanya Reid.
Description: Hauppauge, New York : Nova Science Publisher's, Inc., [2016] | Series: Substance abuse assessment, interventions and treatment | Includes index.
Identifiers: LCCN 2016026172 (print) | LCCN 2016026777 (ebook) | ISBN 9781634856126 (hardcover) | ISBN 9781634856294 (ebook) | ISBN 9781634856294 ()
Subjects: LCSH: Substance abuse--Treatment.
Classification: LCC RC564 .S833 2016 (print) | LCC RC564 (ebook) | DDC 362.29--dc23
LC record available at https://lccn.loc.gov/2016026172

Published by Nova Science Publishers, Inc. † New York

CONTENTS

PREFACE

This book discusses the influences, treatment options and health effects of substance abuse. Chapter One examines the phenomenon of alcoholism and alcoholic psychoses in Russia from the late Soviet to post-Soviet period. Chapter Two studies the validity and reliability of alcohol use data collected via the Amazon's Mechanical Turk (MTurk), a commonly used tool for social science research. Chapter Three assesses and compares certain parameters of sexual functioning in patients with alcohol dependence syndrome. Chapter Four summarizes the results of two double-blind, placebo-controlled pilot studies conducted in order to evaluate the efficacy of mirtazapine for the treatment of persons with comorbid major depressive disorder and alcohol use disorder (MDD/AUD). Chapter Five presents a re-offense prevention program which specifically addresses the participant's social network composition. Chapter Six reviews the epidemiology of the hepatitis B virus infection among non-injecting drug users. Chapter Seven discusses the macro- and micro-level factors that influence the emergence and sustainability of recovery high schools (RHS) and conclude that both grassroots advocates and policy-makers must consider the myriad ecological forces and their influence on the development of particular recovery support programs.

Chapter 1 – Alcoholic psychosis is a secondary psychosis that usually occurs in alcohol-dependent individuals after the prolonged period of heavy drinking and withdrawal. The alcoholic psychoses incidence rates is a reliable indicator of alcohol-related problems at the population level since there is a strong relationship between alcoholic psychoses incidence rates and alcohol consumption per capita. Russia has one of the highest incidences of alcoholism and alcoholic psychoses in Europe, which may be explained by high overall population drinking and prevalence of irregular heavy drinking of vodka. The role of binge drinking of vodka in modifying the effect of alcohol on the risk of alcoholic psychoses in Russia has been emphasized in clinical and aggregate-level studies. This chapter examines the phenomenon of alcoholism and alcoholic psychoses in Russia from the late Soviet to post-Soviet period.

Chapter 2 – Amazon's Mechanical Turk (MTurk) is a commonly used tool for social science research; however, limited research has addressed the validity of data gathered from this online marketplace. The current study examined the validity and reliability of data collected from 1,294 MTurk participants (50.3% female, mean age = 33.4, 81.9% Caucasian) who completed common alcohol research measures, including the UPPS-P Impulsive Behavior Scale – short form (SUPPS-P), the Alcohol Use Disorder Identification Test (AUDIT) and the Timeline Followback (TLFB). Confirmatory factor analysis supported a five-factor structure of the SUPPS-P; internal consistency estimates for all scales were adequate (α's 0.72-0.80). SUPPS-P scales were related as expected with AUDIT (r's 0.10 to 0.20, p's < .005) and total drinks (r's 0.08 to 0.09, p's < .05). As expected, using hierarchical linear regression, urgency traits were significantly related to AUDIT scores ($\Delta R^2 = 0.02$, $p < .001$) over and above other SUPPS-P traits and demographic variables. Our results suggest that MTurk data can be valid and reliable for alcohol and social science research.

Chapter 3 – *Background:* Alcohol dependence syndrome is related to sexual difficulties, e.g., a decrease or a loss of libido, erectile dysfunction, premature ejaculation and a decreased libido. This study was undertaken to assess and compare certain parameters of sexual functioning in patients with alcohol dependence syndrome. *Subjects and methods:* The study population consisted of 106 patients diagnosed with the alcohol dependency syndrome between 26 and 71 years of age who were treated and followed in Psychiatric Hospital Ormož between 2010 and 2012. The patients were followed in hospital and post-hospital setting. An abbreviated version of the Eysenck's Inventory of attitudes to sex was used in this study. *Results:* In the aspect of the libido and pornography there is a significant statistical difference in the field of gender, i.e., men compared to women have an increased libido. In regard to the factor "sexual satisfaction" the post-hospital group shows a greater presence of this factor than the hospital group. As by the libido, regarding the sexual satisfaction there are as well no significant differences among the depressed and the non-depressed patients with the alcohol dependency syndrome – a probable reason lies in the use of antidepressant drugs. *Conclusion:* In the post-hospital group of patients the improvement in attitudes towards the sexuality occurs spontaneously without any specific targeted therapeutic treatment.

Chapter 4 – This report summarizes the results of our two double-blind, placebo-controlled pilot studies conducted in order to evaluate the efficacy of mirtazapine for the treatment of persons with comorbid major depressive disorder and an alcohol use disorder (MDD/AUD). The first of these studies has been completed, but the second study, which involved a younger treatment sample, remains ongoing, so outcome data concerning the second study is mostly limited to a presentation of side effects that have been noted to date in that study. To the authors' knowledge, these were the first two studies to evaluate the efficacy of the novel antidepressant mirtazapine for treating both the depressive symptoms and the level of alcohol consumption of persons with comorbid major depression and an alcohol use disorder (MDD/AUD), since previous studies involving mirtazapine in MDD/AUD did not assess the level of alcohol consumption. Mirtazapine was well tolerated in both of our studies, with few side effects and with no serious adverse events. The results of the first study showed a significant within-group decrease in depressive symptoms by week 2, which was also noted at all subsequent assessments (weeks 3, 4, 6, 8, 10, and 12) during the 12-week study. However, no evidence of efficacy was sound for mirtazapine for decreasing the level of alcohol consumption of MDD/AUD subjects. Also, no significant between-group differences in level of either depressive symptoms or of alcohol consumption was noted in either study, perhaps because of limited sample size. Further studies are warranted to assess the efficacy of mirtazapine for treating comorbid populations.

Chapter 5 – In this chapter, a re-offense prevention program is presented which specifically addresses the participant's social network composition. Beating the Scene, as the program is called, is a protocolized program that makes ample use of cognitive behavioral therapeutic techniques. This program has five main goals: 1: The creation of awareness of the negative influences of the participant's criminogenic peer group, 2: The enhancement of the participant's motivation to build up a prosocial network, 3: The design of a personalized and rewarding prosocial network, 4: The acquisition of the necessary social skills, and 5: The buddy-assisted introduction of participants into existing prosocial networks. Beating the Scene can be used in both inpatient and outpatient settings. It can be added to a wide array of forensic treatment regimens for patients suffering from SUDs.

Chapter 6 – Hepatitis B virus (HBV) is a major cause of cirrhosis and hepatocellular carcinoma, even after introduction of vaccination programs in recent decades. Brazil is considered an area of low prevalence of HBV infections, however has record of high prevalence of HBV infections in locations in the Brazilian Amazon. To date, few epidemiological studies have been conducted on vulnerable populations in the Amazon. This study determined the prevalence and factors associated with HBV infection among non-injecting drug users in the state of Pará, Brazilian Amazon. This was a cross-sectional study conducted in private and public drug-treatment centers in nine municipalities in the state of Pará, Brazilian Amazon. All non-injecting drug users provided information through face-to-face interview. The diagnosis of HBV infection was obtained by EIA and real-time PCR. Simple and multiple logistic regressions were done to assess the risk factors associated with HBV infection. During 2008-2011, 300 non-injecting drug users attending drug-treatment centers participated in this study. Most non-injecting drug users were male (63.7%). The mean age was 32.5 years. The non-injecting drugs most consumed were: crack cocaine, cannabis, and cocaine paste. Tobacco and alcohol were also commonly consumed. In total, 81 (27.0%) non-injecting drug users were exposed to HBV. Being that, 12 users had HBV-DNA. The genotype A (50.0%), D (33.3%) and F (16.7%) were identified. Several risk factors were associated with HBV infection: age ≥35 years, male, tattoos, use of drugs for more than five years, use of drugs everyday, unprotected sex, sexual intercourse with another drug user, involvement in prostitution, and more than 20 sexual partners over the past 2 years. This study identified relevant epidemiological information of HBV infection in non-injecting drug users. It determined a high prevalence of HBV infection, being detected predominance of genotype A. Possibly, the spread of HBV is associated with factors related sexual and parenteral routes and the time of life and drug use.

Chapter 7 – Communities provide a supportive ecology for adolescents in recovery; thus, it is illuminating to explore contextual influences that enable and/or hinder the emergence and sustainability of recovery high schools (RHS) – a recovery support for adolescents working to overcome addiction. In this article, we use ecological mapping to examine the developmental trajectory of RHS in two states where they have proliferated. Using these case studies, we discuss the macro- and micro-level factors that influence the emergence and sustainability of RHS and conclude that both grassroots advocates and policy-makers must consider the myriad ecological forces and their influence on the development of particular recovery support programs.

In: Substance Abuse
Editor: Tanya Reid
ISBN: 978-1-63485-612-6

Chapter 1

ALCOHOLISM AND ALCOHOLIC PSYCHOSES IN RUSSIA

Y. E. Razvodovsky*
Grodno State Medical University, Grodno, Belarus

ABSTRACT

Alcoholic psychosis is a secondary psychosis that usually occurs in alcohol-dependent individuals after the prolonged period of heavy drinking and withdrawal. The alcoholic psychoses incidence rates is a reliable indicator of alcohol-related problems at the population level since there is a strong relationship between alcoholic psychoses incidence rates and alcohol consumption per capita. Russia has one of the highest incidences of alcoholism and alcoholic psychoses in Europe, which may be explained by high overall population drinking and prevalence of irregular heavy drinking of vodka. The role of binge drinking of vodka in modifying the effect of alcohol on the risk of alcoholic psychoses in Russia has been emphasized in clinical and aggregate-level studies. This chapter examines the phenomenon of alcoholism and alcoholic psychoses in Russia from the late Soviet to post-Soviet period.

* Author for correspondence: Grodno State Medical University, 80 Gorky Street, Grodno 230009, Belarus, tel.: + 375 0152 70 18 84, fax: +375 0152 43 53 41, e-mail: razvodovsky@tut.by, yury_razvodovsky@mail.ru.

INTRODUCTION

Alcohol is a neurotoxin that affects the brain in a complex manner through prolonged exposure and repeated withdrawal, resulting in significant morbidity and mortality [5, 43, 44]. Alcohol used disorders associated with alcohol-induced brain damage include: delirium tremens, alcoholic hallucinosis, alcoholic paranoia, Korsakoffs psychosis, alcohol dementia, alcoholic depression [10, 12]. Alcohol-related psychosis is a secondary psychosis occurring in many alcohol-related conditions, including acute intoxication and withdrawal [33, 36]. Alcohol-induced psychotic disorders are characterized by an acute onset of hallucinations and/or delusions that occur either during or after a period of heavy drinking [5, 45]. Psychotic symptoms should be in excess of those usually associated with intoxication or withdrawal syndrome with perceptual disturbances, and symptoms should not persist more than a month during a substance free period [45].

The association between alcohol abuse and psychosis was documented as early as 1847 by Marcel who described "madness as a result of drinking" [17]. Krepelin described this disorder as follows "The picture of disease which has a certain resemblance to delirium tremens, in the fantastic delusions, the vividness of hallucinations, the remarkable combination of insane ideas with a sense of illness and the alcoholic origin [13]. Bleuler described the alcoholic hallucinosis in the following way "Alcoholic insanity is in many respects the opposite to delirium tremens. It manifests itself chiefly in auditory hallucinations, which have a peculiar character: that is they discuss him in the third person; much more rarely they speak to him" [4].

Alcoholic psychosis may occur at any age, but more often in patients aged 35-40 who have abused alcohol for a long time [12]. Therefore, psychosis is usually an indication of chronic alcoholism and is associated with medical, neurological, and psychosocial complications. Approximately 10% of alcohol-dependent patients experience alcohol-induced psychosis [10]. Concurrent dysregulation of several neurotransmitter systems may be involved in the pathogenesis of alcoholic psychosis, and neiro-imaging studies suggest perfusion abnormalities to various brain regions including frontal and temporal lobes, basal ganglia, thalamus [35, 36].

Alcoholic psychosis is associated with high mortality rates [10, 23]. A recent study indicates that mortality among those who have suffered alcohol-induced psychosis is twenty times that of others in the same age group [1]. Mortality was also twelve times higher in the group than of study participants with alcohol dependence alone. Over the eight-year follow-up period of the study, 37% of those who had suffered alcoholic psychosis died [1].

The alcoholic psychoses rate is a reliable indicator of alcohol-related problems at the population level since there is a strong relationship between alcoholic psychoses incidence rates and alcohol consumption per capita [21]. There is also evidence that beverage preference may have modifying influence on the association between alcohol consumption and alcoholic psychoses rates independently of the amount of alcohol consumed. In his pioneering work Wald and Jaroszewski [42] using Polish data reported a close association between the incidence of alcoholic psychoses and consumption of distilled spirits but not with consumption of wine or beer. More recently, Razvodovsky replicates this finding in his time series analysis based on Belarusian [25] and Russian data [30]. The stronger association between alcoholic psychoses incidence rate and vodka sales may be attributable to biological and sociobehavioral mechanisms. A more likely explanation for this finding is that the heavy drinkers tend to prefer spirits as the least expensive form of alcohol [28]. A second possible explanation for these findings is that drinking pattern of spirits users was substantially different from wine or beer users. There is suggestive evidence that consumption of spirits is more closely associated with larger quantities of alcohol consumed per occasion [3].

Some clinical studies have reported that the consumption of particular beverages was related to the appearance of alcoholic psychoses. In his study of case histories of alcohol dependent men, Iliuk and coauthors [11] demonstrated a strong association between the risk of alcoholic psychoses and vodka consumptions. Vodka preference was associated with the consumption of bigger doses of pure ethanol, more severe withdrawal syndrome, more frequent complications, such as the convulsive syndrome and alcoholic psychoses, compared to the beer preference [11]. Another study of outpatients with alcohol dependence revealed that patients who preferred hard liquor during the last month consumed more alcohol in terms of pure ethanol [2]. Also, the period of hard drinking was longer and patients had more social, legal, and psychological problems as well as somatic and psychopathological disorders. Emerging evidence also indicate that binge drinking has profound effects on neurobiological processes in the brain and amplifies the risk of brain damage [43].

Russia ranks among the world's heaviest drinking countries with an annual official consumption rate about 10 litres of pure alcohol per capita [20], while independent estimates show a figure as high as 17 litres [27]. The increase in the death rate in Russia during 1990s was accompanied by a rapid growth in sales of strong spirits (vodka), while the episodic heavy or binge drinking pattern of consumption strong spirits that is commonplace has also been linked to an increased level of alcohol-related morbidity and mortality [15, 19, 26]. Russia has one of the highest incidence of alcoholism and alcoholic psychoses in Europe [2], which may be explained by high overall population drinking and prevalence of irregular heavy drinking of vodka [37, 38]. The role of binge drinking of vodka in modifying the effect of alcohol on the risk of alcoholic psychoses in Russia has been emphasized in clinical and aggregate-level studies [11, 29, 30]. Some estimates suggest that a total number of alcoholics in the late-Soviet Russia was ranging between 23 and 28 millions [35]. Currently, there are approximately 15 million alcoholics in Russia, and the number of heavy drinkers is three to four times that number [20].

The follow-up study of alcoholic psychoses in male patients admitted to a clinical department of a psychiatric hospital indicated that patients with alcoholic psychoses made up from 15 to 30% of all patients [2]. Alcoholic delirium morbidity made up from 69 to 82% of the total number of alcoholic psychoses; alcoholic hallucinosis varied from 14 to 27%. In alcoholic hallucinosis, verbal contrast hallucinations, making comment hallucinations, visual illusions were most frequent. The family history of mental disorders and alcoholism was noted in 30% of patients with alcoholic psychosis [2]. In Russia, like in other countries, alcoholic psychosis is mainly a male phenomenon with a male to female rate ratio of 5:1 [16].

Previous findings based on Russian data suggest that the number of inpatients undergoing treatment for alcoholic psychosis is considered to be one of the most reliable indicators of alcohol-related problems closely correlating with population drinking [25]. At the same time, the number of newly revealed cases of alcoholism shows no correlation with the level of alcohol consumption per capita [25]. Similarly, the number of alcohol-dependent patients registered at state-run narcological establishments (dispensaries) shows no correlation with the level of alcohol consumption per capita [2]. Instead, it correlates positively with the number of doctors-narcologists.

In the present chapter we focused on the aggregate effect of changes in alcohol consumption on alcoholism and alcohol psychoses incidence/ prevalence rates in Russia between 1970 and 2014.

METHODS

Data

We specified the number of alcohol dependent patients without alcoholic psychoses and the number of alcohol dependent patients with alcoholic psychoses, witches were admitted to hospital for the first time as incidence of alcoholism and incidence of alcoholic psychoses (ICD–10: F 10), and the total number of officially registered alcohol dependent patients without alcoholic psychoses and the number of alcohol dependent patients with alcoholic psychoses as prevalence of alcoholism and prevalence of alcoholic psychoses. We also specified the ratio of alcoholic psychoses to alcoholism incidence as Ri and the ratio of alcoholic psychoses to alcoholism prevalence as Rp. The data on alcoholism/alcoholic psychoses incidence/prevalence rates (per 100.000 of the population) and data on per capita alcohol sales are taken from the Russian State Statistical Committee (*Rosstat*) reports (www.gks.ru).

Statistical Analysis

To examine the relation between changes in the sales of alcohol and alcoholism/alcoholic psychoses incidence/prevalence rates across the study period a time-series analysis was performed using the statistical package "Statistica." The dependent variables were the alcoholism/alcoholic psychoses incidence/prevalence rates and the independent variables were alcohol sales. Bivariate correlations between the raw data from two time-series can often be spurious due to common sources in the trends and due to autocorrelation [20]. One way to reduce the risk of obtaining a spurious relation between two variables that have common trends is to remove these trends by means of a 'differencing' procedure, as expressed in formula:

$$\nabla x_t = x_t - x_{t-1}$$

This means that the annual changes '∇' in variable 'X' are analyzed rather than raw data. The process whereby systematic variation within a time series is eliminated before the examination of potential causal relationships is referred to as 'prewhitening.' This is subsequently followed an inspection of the cross-correlation function in order to estimate the association between the two prewhitened time series. It was Box and Jenkins [6] who first proposed this particular method for undertaking a time series analysis and it is commonly referred to as ARIMA modeling. We used this model specification to estimate the relationship between the time series of alcohol sales per capita and alcoholism/alcoholic psychoses incidence/prevalence rates in this paper.

RESULTS

The trends in the alcoholic psychoses incidence/prevalence rates are displayed in Figure 1. As can be seen, the alcoholic psychoses incidence/prevalence rates fluctuated greatly over the period: increased subctantially during the 1970s, decreased markedly from 1980 to 1984, dropped sharply between 1984-1987, than started on an upward trend from 1987-1992, before jumping dramatically during 1992 to 1995. From 1995-1998 there was a fall in the rates before they again jumping between 1998 and 2003 and then started to decrease in the most recent years.

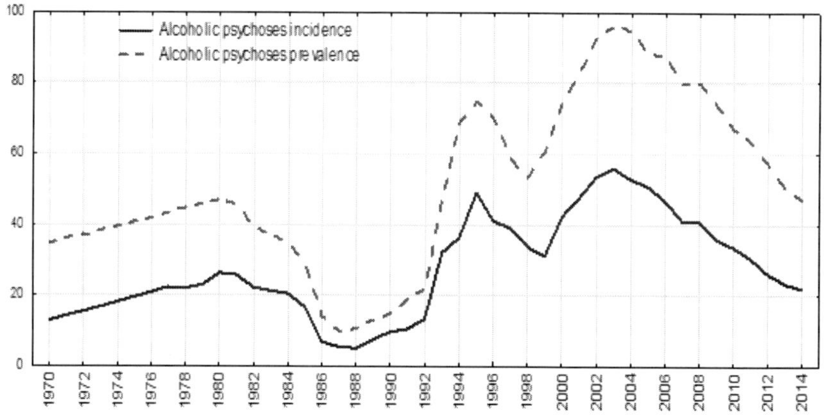

Figure 1. Trends in alcoholic psychoses incidence/prevalence rates in Russia between 1970 and 2014.

The trends in the alcoholism incidence/prevalence rates is displayed in Figure 2. The incidence of alcoholism increased dramatically during 1970s reaching its peak in 1980, than dropped sharply between 1987 and 1992. There were also spikes in the incidence of alcoholism in 1994 and 2003. Similar temporal pattern demonstrated the prevalence of alcoholism. This index increased rapidly reaching its peak in 1987 and then started to decrease. The trends in the ratio Ri and Rp were rather similar to the alcoholic psychoses incidence/prevalence trends (Figure 3). The graphical evidence suggests that the temporal pattern of alcoholism and alcoholic psychoses incidence rates differ markedly (Figure 4).

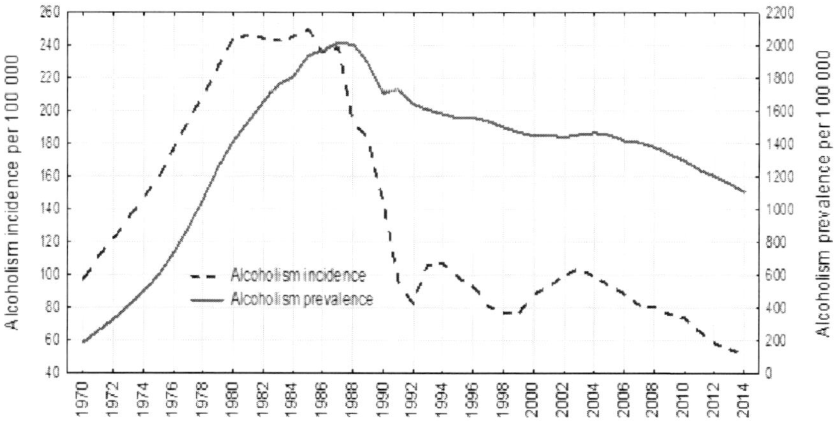

Figure 2. Trends in alcoholism incidence/prevalence rates in Russia between 1970 and 2014.

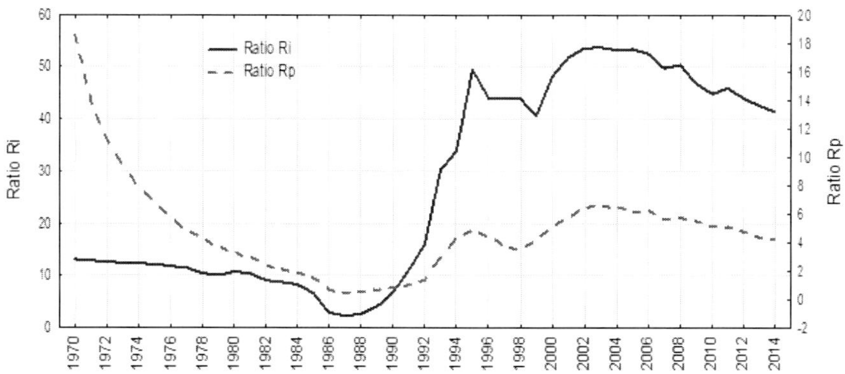

Figure 3. Trends in ratio Ri and Rp in Russia between 1970 and 2014.

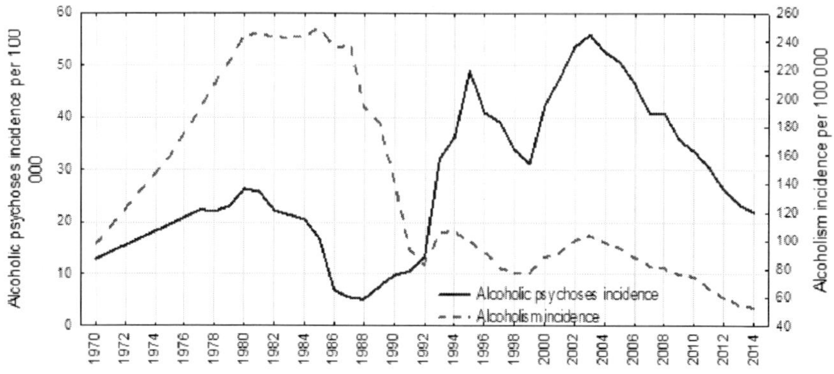

Figure 4. Trends in alcoholism and alcoholic psychoses incidence rates in Russia between 1970 and 2014.

The average per capita alcohol sales figure was 8.7 liters with vodka being the drink overwhelmingly consumed. The temporal pattern of alcohol sales per capita in Russia is shown in Figure 5. As can be seen, the alcohol sales have experienced sharp fluctuations across the period. Thus, a brief Andropov's anti-alcohol campaign in the early 1980s resulted in a decline in alcohol sales. An especially sharp fall was recorded in alcohol sales in 1985-1987 that coincided with Mikhail Gorbachev's anti-alcohol campaign. Similarly, the collapse of the Soviet Union and the ending of the state's alcohol monopoly in the early 1990s were accompanied by a sharp rise in alcohol sales.

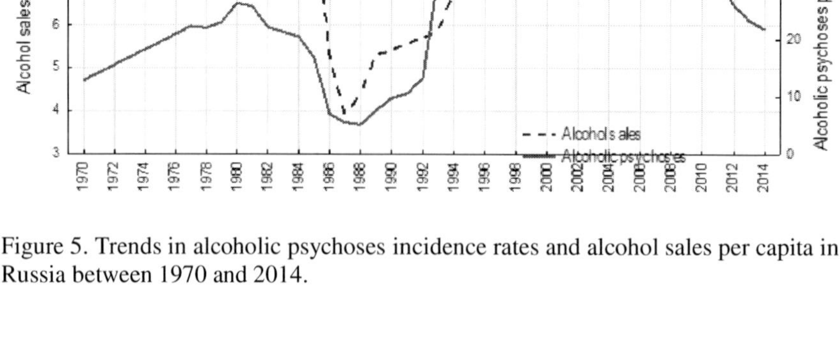

Figure 5. Trends in alcoholic psychoses incidence rates and alcohol sales per capita in Russia between 1970 and 2014.

The graphical evidence suggests that the temporal pattern of alcoholic psychoses incidence/prevalence rates fits closely with changes in alcohol sales per capita (Figures 5-7). At the same time, trends in alcoholism incidence/prevalence and alcohol sales differ markedly (Figures 6-8). There were sharp trends in the time series data across the study period. These trends were removed by means of a first-order differencing procedure. After prewhitening the cross-correlations between the alcoholism and alcoholic psychoses incidence/prevalence rates and alcohol sales were inspected. This indicated that there was a statistically significant cross-correlation between per capita alcohol sales and alcoholic psychoses incidence/prevalence as well as ratio Ri and Rp at lag zero. At the same time, there was no cross-correlation between the level of alcohol sales and alcoholism incidence/prevalence rates.

Table 1. Estimated effects (bivariate ARIMA model) of alcohol sales on alcoholism and alcoholic psychoses incidence/prevalence rates

Parameter	Model	Estim.	St. Error	P
Alc. psychoses incidence	0.1.0*	0.176	0.031	0.000
Alcoholism incidence	0.1.0	0.004	0.020	0.858
Alc. psychoses prevalence	0.1.0	0.140	0.028	0.000
Alcoholism prevalence	0.1.0	0.004	0.017	0.811
Ratio Ri	0.1.0	0.172	0.030	0.000
Ratio Rp	0.1.0	0.136	0.034	0.000

*The general form of non-seasonal ARIMA model is (p,d,q), where p - the order of the autoregressive parameter, d – the order of differencing, and q – the order of the moving average parameter. Q test for residuals are satisfactory in all models.

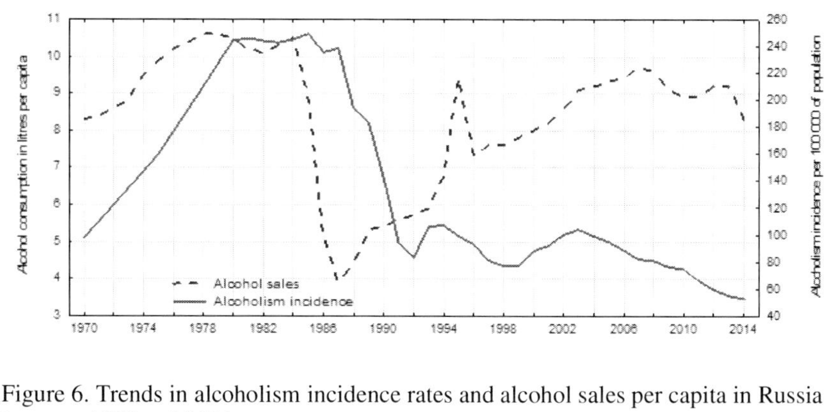

Figure 6. Trends in alcoholism incidence rates and alcohol sales per capita in Russia between 1970 and 2014.

Figure 7. Trends in alcoholic psychoses prevalence rates and alcohol sales per capita in Russia between 1970 and 2014.

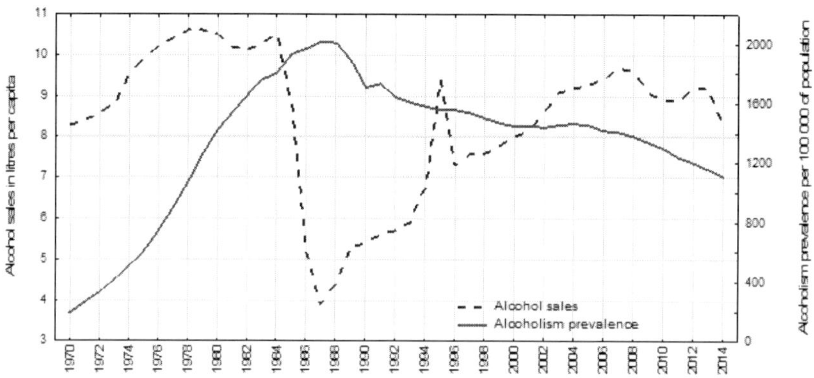

Figure 8. Trends in alcoholism prevalence rates and alcohol sales per capita in Russia between 1970 and 2014.

The specification of the bivariate ARIMA model and outcome of the analyses are presented in Table 1. According to the results, alcohol sales is a statistically significant associated with alcoholic psychoses incidence/ prevalence rates, implying that a 1-litre increase in per capita alcohol sales is associated with an increase in the alcoholic psychoses incidence/prevalence rates of 17.6% and 14.0% correspondingly. The analysis also suggests that alcohol sales were associated with ratio Ri and Rp. The estimated effects of alcohol sales on both coefficients are clearly statistically significant: a 1 liter increase in alcohol sales would result in a 17.2% in the ratio Ri and 13.6% increase in the ratio Rp. The association between alcohol sales per capita and alcoholism incidence/prevalence rates was also positive, but statistically not significant.

Discussion

According to the results of present analysis there was a positive and statistically significant effect of per capita alcohol sales on alcoholic psychoses incidence/prevalence rates in Russia. These results are consistent with the previous findings that highlighted close temporal association between alcoholic psychoses rate and population drinking [21, 42]. It should be emphasis that the results suggest a fairly quick response of alcoholic psychoses incidence/prevalence rates to changes in population drinking. The instantaneous response in morbidity rate from chronic alcohol-related diseases seem quite surprising when considering the long latency period at the individual level. There are, however, reasonable explanations for this seeming inconsistency. It seems plausible that in a population there exists a reservoir of heavy drinkers who are near the critical threshold-value for developing alcoholic psychosis. In case when these high risk individuals increase alcohol consumption, they will exceed the threshold value and this can contribute to the development of psychosis. This is the reason why the immediate impact on chronic alcohol-related diseases can be registered from marked changes in aggregate consumption.

Elucidating the phenomenon of high alcoholic psychoses incidence/ prevalence rates in Russia, however, does little to understand the reasons for it dramatic fluctuations across time. Recent Russian history can be divided into several major periods: 1) the late-Soviet period of general stagnation, associated with Brezhnev era; 2) the period of perestroika and Gorbachev's anti-alcohol campaign in the mid-1980s; 3) the political and economic transition following the breakup of the Soviet Union in 1991; 4) the worsening economic situation associated with financial crisis in 1998; 5) the period of economic growth over the last decade. The trends in alcoholic psychoses incidence/prevalence coincide with these major social events.

During the last decades, Soviet and later Russian governments adopted a series of measures in an attempt to curb the alcohol-related burden. In 1972 a resolution by the CPSU Central Committee "About the Measures Restricting Alcohol Consumption" was passed [20]. According to the document, the production of vodka and the number of shops selling it were to be cut. In 1974, the RSFSR Supreme Soviet ratified a decree creating a system of institutions (medical-labor dispensaries) within the Ministry of Internal Affaires for the long-term compulsory treatment of advanced alcoholics manifesting antisocial behavior [18].

Despite these efforts, during the 1970s, there was a dramatic growth in the incidence and prevalence of alcohol dependence reported by official statistics. To some extent this growth reflects the active development of the narcological service, which was officially created in 1976 according to the Order of the Ministry of Health of the USSR №131 [20]. Before 1976, narcological assistance to alcohol-dependent patients was made by psychiatrists in the structure of general psychiatric clinic. Since 1976, the narcological service grew rapidly, reaching its peak of funding and access to resources during the antialcohol campaign in 1985-1988. This led to the creation of the narcological in-patient and out-patient departments, as well an increase in the number of specialists in the field of narcology [16].

One of the most intriguing aspects of Russian alcohol history is the substantial decline in alcohol consumption and alcohol-related morbidity/ mortality rates that occurred between 1980 and 1984. Nemtsov argues that this decline was most likely due to the creation of three new services: medical-labour dispensaries and narcological and resuscitation services [16]. According to him, the impact of these measures only became visible after the passage of several years because of organizational difficulties. There is, however, an alternative explanation for this phenomenon which might be partially attributed to the increase in the price of vodka in 1981 [20]. Furthermore, the new Soviet leader Andropov, who came to power in 1982, realized that mass drunkenness was a major threat to the Soviet system and saw a great opportunity to increase labor productivity by sobering up the nation. He took a number of steps in this direction using police methods to strengthen labor discipline and to fight against drunkenness in the workplace [16]. His successor, Chernenko, expressed concern over the failure of earlier campaigns to effect changes in the population's drinking habits and began to make plans for a national antialcohol movement. There is evidence that official policies were beginning to bear fruit during the early 1980s: both per capita alcohol consumption and the alcoholic psychoses incidence/prevalence rates was falling.

Gorbachev's anti-alcohol campaign in the 1985-1988 is the most well-known natural experiment in the field of alcohol policy [20]. It seems obvious that sudden decline in alcoholic psychosis prevalence during this time appears to be entirely due to anti-alcohol campaign that significantly reduced alcohol consumption by limiting its manufacture and availability.

The collapse of the Soviet Union and the ending of the state's alcohol monopoly in January 1992 were accompanied by a sharp rise in alcohol sales [16]. Treisman argue that the increase in alcohol consumption in the early 1990s, which explains much of the rise in mortality, resulted largely from an increase in the affordability of vodka [40]. With price liberalization in 1992, vodka became much more affordable because of a dramatic drop in its relative price. In the period from 1995 the real vodka price recovered somewhat until 1998, after which point the trend turned down again [20]. After 1998, alcoholic psychoses rate increased as well.

It should be emphasized that alcohol sales per capita before the start of antialcohol campaign exceeded the level recorded in the early 1990s, while alcoholic psychoses incidence/prevalence rates in the early 1990s exceeded the level of early 1980s significantly. This means that some additional factors came into play in the yearly 1990s. Some experts have underlined the importance of the effect of the psychosocial distress of economic and political reforms as the main reason for the mortality crisis in Russia in the early 1990s [8]. In this period Russia faced a deep socioeconomic crisis accompanied by unemployment grows, hyperinflation, dramatic decline in the well-being of the majority of the population [39]. The turmoil associated with socioeconomic and political transition affected Russian peoples and lead to the high prevalence of poverty, poor nutrition and adverse health behavior such as binge drinking and smoking [9]. In particular, rapid mass privatization and increased unemployment rate was suggested as the major determinant of the mortality crisis in Russia in the early 1990s [39]. Similarly, the dramatic rise in alcoholic psychoses incidence rates between 1998 and 2003 may be associated with the financial crisis which resulted in hyperinflation, increasing poverty, political and economic uncertainty [20].

Several studies have shown that unemployment have adverse effects on physical and mental health [7, 8]. It was also assumed that this association is mediated through psychosocial distress, which leads to the adoption of unhealthy lifestyle including smoking and hazardous drinking [8]. In relation to this, it should be emphasized that alcoholics seem to respond to many life events by being stressed. It appears that given approximately equal amounts of stress, the alcoholics report more perceived stress than nonalcoholics [7]. Since alcoholics seem to perceive more stress, it follows that they must also perceive less control or fewer alternatives for coping. This suggests that psychosocial stress may be more strongly associated with increased risk for binge drinking in alcoholics than in nonalcoholics. Clinical observations and epidemiological studies also reported an association between self-perceived stress and risk of relapse [9]. The increased demand for alcohol in Russia in the early-1990s attributed to psychosocial distress was met by factors that increased supply following the repeal of the state alcohol monopoly in January 1992 [20].

It is possible that increase in alcoholic psychoses prevalence rate in Russia in the mid-1990s, at least partly, is a consequence of deterioration in the quality of health care system, following the collapse of Soviet Union in late 1991. A process of destruction of the state-funded narcological service that began in 1989 continued in the 1990s [20]. During the 1990s, several important changes linked to broader post-Soviet socioeconomic transformation had significant effect on the addiction treatment system. In connection with the dismantling of the Soviet administrative economy generally and the restructuring of the health care sector in particular, the narcological service experienced the budgetary cutbacks. In relation to this the total number of hospital beds has decreased and the length of stay in hospital has shortened [14]. Shortages of medications and stuff were also common. During this time state-run narcological service found themselves competing with an "alternative medicine" and a number of movements like Alcoholic Anonymous [24]. Other changes came with the abolishment of compulsory treatment laws and the commercialization of narcology. This commercialization was directly linked to treatment methods such as "chemical isolation" (implantation of disulfiram), and emotional-stress psychotherapy or "kodirovanie" which represented the main sources of additional income for physicians working in the state-run network [24]. Many other aspects of addiction treatment in Russia had been radically transformed during the 1990s. In particular, anonymous forms of treatment have become much more popular [14]. It should be noted that these changes could be partially explained by a shift in treatment practices from long-term to short-term in-patients treatment and from in-patient to out-patient treatment.

It seems plausible that dramatic increase in alcoholic psychoses incidence/prevalence rates in the mid-1990s was to a great extent due to changed alcohol consumption structure, when 80% of all alcohol in Russia was consumed in the form of spirits. Furthermore, despite the recent growth in the consumption of beer, vodka continues to be the beverage that dominates in terms of consumption [20].

The phenomenon of fortified wine consumption, mainly related to the Soviet period, might be a potential confounding factor in the temporal association between per capita alcohol sales and the alcoholic psychoses incidence rates in Russia. Cheap fortified wines with relatively high alcohol content became especially popular among alcoholics in the 1970s [41]. According to a survey conducted among alcohol-dependent individuals in this period, about 80% of them regularly consumed fortified wines [16]. Fortified wines were generally consumed without meals in order to achieve a rapid intoxication effect. Some commentators believe that fortified wines were more harmful than vodka, causing deeper intoxication and a severe hangover, because the quality of the spirits added to fortified wines was generally poor [16]. Unfortunately, this speculation is not supported by scientific evidence, as no toxicological evaluation was carried out in order to determine whether fortified wine consumption carried a health risk.

Available evidence suggests that during the Soviet period the trend was away from low alcohol content table wines (dry and semi-dry with a 10, 5–11, 5% average alcohol content) in favor of stronger fortified wines (14.5% for dessert wine and 18.5% for strong wine) [41]. According to Soviet statistics between 1955 and 1979 the supply of grape wine available for domestic consumption increased 7.9 times (from 461 to 3635 million litres), while the supply of fortified wines increased 17.8 times (from 130 to 2315 million litres) [16]. It appears, however, that consumption of fortified wine was falling by the early 1980s before almost completely disappearing during Gorbachev's anti-alcohol campaign [20]. These data indicate that fortified wine was the key beverage driving the sharp fall in recorded alcohol consumption in Russia during the anti-alcohol campaign. The substantial drop in wine sales during this period resulted in the unfavorable shift in the structure of alcohol consumption from wine towards vodka in the 1990s, which was associated with a dramatic growth in the alcoholic psychoses incidence/prevalence rates.

Another potential reason for the detrimental effect of alcohol on alcoholic psychoses incidence/prevalence rates was deterioration of his quality. According to the data from the State Statistics Service, up to 45% of vodka sold during that period did not meet quality standards [20]. Furthermore, unrecorded consumption of alcohol was commonplace in Russia throughout the study period, especially in the mid-1990s, when a considerable proportion of vodka came from illicit sources [32]. The consumption of homemade spirits (samogon) and surrogates might also have a particularly negative impact on alcohol-related morbidity and morbidity [15].

Official statistics appear to show a gradual decrease in the incidence and prevalence of alcohol dependence since 1987. However, many experts believe that these trends are misleading and that the incidence/prevalence of alcohol dependence are actually increasing [14, 20]. The fact that official statistics on alcohol dependence are misleading could be attributable to degradation and disorganization of narcological service. It should be stated that the rates of alcoholism incidence is influenced by a number of factors. In particular, it is influenced by sharp decrease in the number of state-run narcological clinics and doctors-narcologists [24]. Besides, due expansion of anonymous forms of treatment, a significant part of alcoholics failed to get registered at narcological dispensaries. At the same time, patients with alcoholic psychosis practically always get into doctor's eyeshot, as they undergo in-patient treatment in state-run narcological service.

In contemporary Russia, recognizing the central role of alcohol in the mortality crisis President Putin signed the laws regulating production and sale of alcohol production in 2005 [18]. These laws contained regulations aimed at controlling the volume and quality of alcohol products and requiring the registration of alcohol production and distribution facilities. The first one (102--FL), among other issues, introduced new excise stamps from January 1st 2006. After that time, other stamps have been prohibited. The second law (209--FL) significantly increased nominal capital of alcohol market players since July 1, 2006, so that the market became free from small and average players in favor of large producers. Moreover, the law 209-introduced new and more toxic denaturant additives for household alcohol-containing liquids after July 1, 2006 [20].

Since 2003, Russia has experienced steep decline in the alcoholic psychoses incidence rate which might be attributed to the implementation of the alcohol policy reforms, which increased government control over the alcohol market [31]. This empirical evidence suggest that recent Russian government's attempt to curb the high alcohol-related morbidity and mortality have been at least partially successful and provide additional evidence that pricing policy may be an effective strategy to reduce an alcohol-related burden. There is, however, some doubts that recent decline in alcoholic psychoses rates in Russia is fully attributable to the alcohol control measures, since downward trend in alcoholic psychoses rates started before decline in recorded alcohol consumption.

CONCLUSION

In conclusion, this study highlighted close temporal association between alcoholic psychoses incidence/prevalence rates and population drinking in Russia. These findings suggest that the alcoholic psychoses incidence/ prevalence rates are the reliable indicators of alcohol-related problems at the population level. The results of this study also indicate, that ratio Ri and Rp are considered to be indexes of the efficiency of narcological service regarding early diagnosing and treatment for alcohol dependence. The higher ratio is, the bigger is the number of alcohol-dependent patients getting into doctor's eyeshot due to alcoholic psychosis, i.e., at late stages of the disease. The outcomes of this study provide indirect support for the hypothesis that the dramatic fluctuations in the alcoholic psychoses incidence rates in Russia during the last decades were related to the availability/affordability of alcohol. The findings from the present study have important implications as regards alcohol policy, suggesting that any attempts to reduce alcohol-related burden should be linked with efforts through restriction of availability/affordability of alcohol.

REFERENCES

[1] Achté K, Seppälä K, Ginman L, Colliander N,Railo J. Alcoholic psychoses in Finland. Helsinki, Finland: Finnish Foundation for Alcohol Studies; 1969.

[2] Aleksin DS, Egorov AY. (2011). Current peculiarities of alcoholic psychosis. *Zh Nevrol Psikhiatr Im S S Korsakova.*111(11):20–7.

[3] Anderson P., Baumberg B. Alcohol in Europe. London: Institute of Alcohol Studies. 2006.

[4] Bleuler E. Textbook of Psychiatry, New York, Macmillan. 1916.

[5] Bouzyk-Szutkiewicz J, Waszkiewicz N, Szulc A. (2012). Alcohol and psychiatric disorders. *Pol Merkur Lekarski.* 33(195):176–81.

[6] Box GEP, Jenkins GM. Time Series Analysis: forecasting and control. London. Holden-Day Inc. 1976.

[7] Brady KT, Sonne SC. (1999). The Role of Stress in Alcohol Use, Alcoholism Treatment, and Relapse *Alcohol Research & Health.* 23(4): 263-271.

[8] Brainerd E, & Cutler DM. (2005). Autopsy on an Empire: Understanding mortality in Russia and the former Soviet Union. *Journal of Economic Perspective.* 19(1):107–130.

[9] Fox HC, Bergquist KL, Hong KI, Sinha R. (2007). Stress-induced and alcohol cue-induced craving in recently abstinent alcohol-dependent individuals. *Alcoholism: Clinical and Experimental Research* 31(3):395–403.

[10] Greenberg DM, Lee JWY. (2001). Psychotic manifestations of alcoholism. *Current Psychiatry Reports*. 3:314-318.

[11] Iliuk RD, Rybakova KV, Kiselev AS, Krupitskiĭ EM. (2011). Epidemiology, medical and social features of the addiction to beer and strong alcohol. *Zh Nevrol Psikhiatr Im S S Korsakova*. 111(11):3–13.

[12] Jordaan GP, Emsley R. (2014). Alcohol-induced psychotic disorder: a review. *Metab Brain Dis*. 29(2):231–43.

[13] Kraepelin E. Lectures on Clinical Psychiatry. London, Bailliere Tindall, 1913.

[14] Krasnov VN, Gurovich I. (2012). History and current condition of Russian psychiatry. *International Review of Psychiatry*. (4):328–333.

[15] Leon D, Saburova L, Tomkins S, Andreev E, Kiryanov N, McKee M, & Shkolnikov V. (2007). Hazardous alcohol drinking and premature mortality in Russia: a population based case-control study. *Lancet*. 369:2001–2009.

[16] Lisitsyn YP, Sidorov PI. (1990) Alcoholism: medico-social aspects. Moscow, Medicine.

[17] Marcel CNS. De la folie causee par l'abus des boissons alcooliques, Thesis, Rignoux, imprimeur de la faculte de medicin, 1847.

[18] Nemtsov A, Razvodovsky YE. (2015). Russian alcohol situation in false mirror. *Sobriology*. 3:70-73.

[19] Nemtsov AV, Razvodovsky YE. (2008). Alcohol situation in Russia, 1980-2005. *Social and Clinical Psychiatry*. 2:52–60.

[20] Nemtsov AV. A contemporary history of alcohol in Russia. Stockholm. Sodertorns hogskola. 2011.

[21] Nemtsov AV, Nechaev AK, Panchenko LA. (1989). Alcohol consumption and alcoholic psychoses. *Zh Nevropatol Psikhiatr Im S S Korsakova.*; 89(2):93–7.

[22] Norström T, Skog OJ. (2001). Alcohol and mortality: methodological and analytical issue in aggregate analysis. *Addiction*. 96:5–17.

[23] Perälä J, Kuoppasalmi K, Pirkola S, Härkänen T, Saarni S, Tuulio-Henriksson A, et al. (2010). Alcohol-induced psychotic disorder and delirium in the general population. *Br J Psychiatry*. 197(3):200–206.

[24] Raikhel E. (2010). Post-Soviet Placebos: Epistemology and Authority in Russian Treatments for Alcoholism. *Cult Med Psychiatry*.34:132–168.

[25] Razvodovsky YE. (2002). Alcoholism and alcoholic psychosis in Belarus in 1970-1999. *Zh Nevrol Psikhiatr Im S S Korsakova*. 102(10):58–63.

[26] Razvodovsky YE. (2010). Beverage specific alcohol sale and mortality in Russia. *Alcoholism.* 46(2), 63–75.

[27] Razvodovsky YE. (2013). Estimation of the level of alcohol consumption in Russia. *ICAP Periodic Review Drinking and Culture.* 8, 6–10.

[28] Razvodovsky YE. (2013). Consumption of noncommercial alcohol among alcohol dependent patients. *Psychiatry Journal* Article ID 691050.

[29] Razvodovsky YE. (2015) Alcoholic psychoses in Russia and Belarus: a comparative analysis of trends. *Alcoholism & Drug Dependence.* 3,4.1-5.

[30] Razvodovsky YE. (2015) The effect of beverage type on alcoholic psychoses rate in Russia. *Alcohol & Alcoholism* 50(2): 200-2005.

[31] Razvodovsky YE. (2014). Was the mortality decline in Russia attributable to alcohol control policy? *Journal of Sociolomics.* 3:2.

[32] Razvodovsky YE. Noncommercial alcohol in central and eastern Europe, ICAP Review 3. In: International Center for Alcohol Policies, ed. *Noncommercial alcohol in three regions.* Washington, DC: ICAP, 2008;17–23.

[33] Schuckit MA, Tipp JE, Reich T, Hesselbrock VM, Bucholz KK. (1995). The histories of withdrawal convulsions and delirium tremens in 1648 alcohol dependent subjects. *Addiction*; 90:1335–1347.

[34] Segal BM. The drunken society – alcohol abuse and alcoholism in the Soviet Union. New York: *Hippocrene Books.* 1990.

[35] Soyka M, Koch W, Tatsch K. (2005). Thalamic hypofunction in alcohol hallucinosis:FDG PET findings. *Psychiatry Research: Neuroimaging* 2005: 139:259-262.

[36] Soyka M. Pathophysiological mechanisms possibly involved in the development of alcohol hallucinosis. *Addiction.* 90:289-294.

[37] Stickley A, Leinsalu M, Andreew E, Razvodovsky YE, Vagero D, McKee M. (2007). Alcohol poisoning in Russia and the countries in the European part of the former Soviet Union, 1970-2002. *European Journal of Public Health*;17(5), 444–449.

[38] Stickley A, Razvodovsky Y, McKee M. (2009). Alcohol and mortality in Russia: A historical perspective. *Public Health.* 23: 20–26.

[39] Stuckler D, King L, Mskee M. (2009). Mass privatization and post-communist mortality crisis: a cross-national analysis. *Lancet.* 373:399-407.

[40] Treisman D. (2010). Death and price. The political economy of Russia's alcohol crisis. *Economics of Transition.*18 (2): 281–331.

[41] Treml V.G. (1982) Alcohol in the USSR. A statistical study. Duke University Press. Durham, N.C.

[42] Wald I, Jaroszewski Z. (1983). Alcohol consumption and alcoholic psychoses in Poland. *Journal of studies on Alcohol* 44(6):1040–8.

[43] Welcome MO, Razvodovsky YE, Pereverzeva EV, Pereverzev VA. (2014). Cognitive functions and neuropsychological status of medical students with different attitudes to alcohol use: a study conducted at the Belarusian State Medical University, Minsk, Belarus. *Physiol Behav* 10(128):108–13.

[44] World Health Organization. Global status report on alcohol and health. Geneva: World Health organization; 2014.

[45] World Health Organization. The ICD-10 Classification of Mental and Behavioural Disorders: Diagnostic Criteria for Research, Geneva, 1993.

In: Substance Abuse
Editor: Tanya Reid

ISBN: 978-1-63485-612-6

Chapter 2

EVIDENCE FOR THE VALIDITY AND RELIABILITY OF ALCOHOL USE DATA COLLECTED VIA AMAZON'S MECHANICAL TURK

Miji Um*, BS, Alexandra R. Hershberger, MS, J. Davis Vander Veen, MS, and Melissa A. Cyders, PhD
Indiana University-Purdue University Indianapolis,
Indianapolis, IN, US

ABSTRACT

Amazon's Mechanical Turk (MTurk) is a commonly used tool for social science research; however, limited research has addressed the validity of data gathered from this online marketplace. The current study examined the validity and reliability of data collected from 1,294 MTurk participants (50.3% female, mean age = 33.4, 81.9% Caucasian) who completed common alcohol research measures, including the UPPS-P Impulsive Behavior Scale – short form (SUPPS-P), the Alcohol Use Disorder Identification Test (AUDIT) and the Timeline Followback (TLFB). Confirmatory factor analysis supported a five-factor structure of the SUPPS-P; internal consistency estimates for all scales were adequate (α's 0.72-0.80). SUPPS-P scales were related as expected with AUDIT

* Corresonding author: Miji Um. E-mail: miji.um@gmail.com.

(r's 0.10 to 0.20, p's $< .005$) and total drinks (r's 0.08 to 0.09, p's $< .05$). As expected, using hierarchical linear regression, urgency traits were significantly related to AUDIT scores ($\Delta R^2 = 0.02$, $p < .001$) over and above other SUPPS-P traits and demographic variables. Our results suggest that MTurk data can be valid and reliable for alcohol and social science research.

Keywords: MTurk, UPPS-P, AUDIT, TLFB, reliability, validity, alcohol

Introduction

Amazon's Mechanical Turk (MTurk; www.mturk.com) is an online marketplace where "workers" earn money by participating in "Human Intelligence Tasks" (HITs) made available by "requesters." Recently, MTurk has gained considerable attention from social scientists given its practicality in participant recruitment and low cost compared to conventional data collection methods (Goodman, Cryder, & Cheema, 2013; Paolacci & Chandler, 2014). However, despite its emerging popularity, particularly in alcohol research (Boynton & Richman, 2014; Hershberger, Karyadi, VanderVeen, & Cyders, 2016; Lovett, Ham, & Veilleux, 2015), little work has addressed the validity of the data gathered from this online marketplace. The goal of this paper is to directly examine the validity and reliability of data gathered from MTurk samples. Although likely generalizable to other questionnaires and surveys, we examine three common and frequently used measures in alcohol research: The UPPS-P Impulsive Behavior Scale-short form (SUPPS-P; Cyders, Littlefield, Coffey, & Karyadi, 2014; Lynam, 2013), the Alcohol Use Disorder Identification Test (AUDIT, Saunders, Aasland, Babor, de la Fuente, & Grant, 1993), and the Timeline Followback calendar (TLFB, Sobell & Sobell, 1992).

Rationale for Using MTurk for Social Science Research

In social science research, conventional data collection frequently utilizes college student samples (Peterson, 2001); however, this methodology is often criticized because college students are a relatively homogenous group in terms of age and educational level and they do display systematic differences from non-student populations (Peterson, 2001). Often, community samples are utilized to overcome these limitations associated with college student samples, as community samples are less homogeneous; however, the major downfalls of collecting data from a community sample are that these samples are harder to recruit and the cost and time associated with recruitment are often high (i.e., newspaper advertisement, monetary compensation for research participation; Berinsky, Huber, & Lenz, 2012).

To this end, MTurk has recently emerged as a novel data collection tool that has several strengths compared to other conventional data collection methods, including rapid data collection, cost-effectiveness, and convenience to the participants (Buhrmester, Kwang, & Gosling, 2011; Goodman et al., 2013). In addition to these benefits, the quality of data from MTurk samples has been proposed to be comparable to those collected through conventional methods (Buhrmester, Kwang, & Gosling, 2011). Generally, MTurk workers from the United States are fairly equally split between men and women (female = 54%), are approximately 32.64 years old (SD = 11.63), most often report Caucasian race (83.5%; Shapiro, Chandler, & Mueller, 2013), and endorse some college education (38.8%) or a college degree (31.8%). MTurk workers from the United States have been found to be more representative of the US general population than college student samples with respect to gender, race, age and education (Paolacci, Chandler, & Ipeirotis, 2010).

Given these strengths, MTurk has recently been used to recruit participants for an array of clinical psychological research, including studies on body image (Gardner, Brown, & Boice, 2012), eating disorders (Farrell, Lee, & Deacon, 2015), depression (Hallford & Mellor, 2016), attention deficit hyperactivity disorder (Wymbs & Dawson, 2015), non-suicidal self-injury disorder (Andover, 2014), and obsessive-compulsive disorder (Fergus & Bardeen, 2014). Notably, Mturk has gained large popularity for assessing alcohol and substance use (Boynton & Richman, 2014; Hershberger, Karyadi, VanderVeen, & Cyders, 2016; VanderBroek, Acker, Palmer, de Wit, & MacKillop, 2015), including daily alcohol consumption (Boynton & Richman, 2014), electronic cigarette use and beliefs (Hershberger et al., 2016), and alcohol effects (Lac & Berger, 2013). However, despite this growing popularity, there is minimal data directly examining the validity and reliability of data gathered from MTurk samples. This is the goal of the current study. Because of MTurk's notable popularity in alcohol use research, we examine, as an example, the validity and reliability of data gathered on three commonly used measures in alcohol use research: The SUPPS-P (Cyders et al., 2014; Lynam, 2013), the AUDIT (Saunders et al., 1993), and the TLFB (Sobell & Sobell, 1992). Establishing that MTurk is a viable and valid way to assess these measures would not only advance alcohol research, but would also suggest viability of MTurk data to answer a wide range of questions pertaining to social science research in a cost-effective, time efficient, and more representative way than using other samples of convenience (e.g., college student samples). In order to reach the study goal, we hypothesized that 1) TLFB, AUDIT scores, and SUPPS-P factors would show good internal consistency, 2) A 5-factor structure of the SUPPS-P would emerge in the MTurk sample (as previously supported by Cyders et al., 2014), and 3) TLFB, AUDIT scores, and SUPPS-P factors would be significantly related as suggested by previous work (Coskunpinar, Dir, & Cyders, 2013).

METHODS

Participants

Data were collected from N = 1,564 participants using Amazon's MTurk in January (n = 743) and April of 2015 (n = 821). Inclusion criteria were: 21 years or older, able to read and understand questions in English, live in the United States, and drink alcohol. Additionally, anyone failing two or more careless responding checks (described below) were removed from data analysis (n = 51 and n = 88, respectively in the two samples) resulting in a sample size of N = 1397. Anyone scoring 3 *SD* above or below the mean on AUDIT, TLFB, or SUPPS-P were removed from analyses, as determined *a priori*, and n = 6 participants were missing all SUPPS-P data, leaving a final sample of N = 1294 (mean age = 33.44, *SD* = 10.64, 50.3% female, 81.9% Caucasian). Participants removed did not differ from the remaining sample in age or gender (p's .18 to .96).

Measures

Alcohol Use

Problematic alcohol consumption was assessed using the Alcohol Use Disorder Identification Test (AUDIT; Saunders et al., 1993). The AUDIT is a ten-item scale that assesses hazardous alcohol consumption, abnormal alcohol consumption behavior, and alcohol related problems. AUDIT responses have previously been shown to demonstrate great psychometric properties (Donovan, Kivlahan, Doyle, Longabaugh, & Greenfield, 2006; Shields & Caruso, 2003).

Total number of drinks was assessed using The Timeline Followback (TLFB; Sobell & Sobell, 1992), which aids participants in estimating daily alcohol consumption. Participants were asked to indicate the number of drinks they consumed each day over a two-week period. Total number of drinks was calculated by summing the total number of drinks each individual consumed over the two-week period. Amount of drinking quantified by TLFB is related to alcohol-related problems (Rueger, Trela, Palmeri, & King, 2012) and treatment outcomes (Guth et al., 2008; Hoeppner, Stout, Jackson, & Barnett, 2010) Responses on the TLFB have been shown to have adequate test-retest reliability for days abstinent from alcohol, days with alcohol consumption and without a binge episode, and days with binge episodes in social drinkers (Sobell & Sobell, 1992). The TLFB also demonstrates high convergent validity with the Addiction Severity Index (Kline, 1998).

Impulse Related Personality Traits

The UPPS-P Impulsive Behavior Scale-short form (SUPPS-P; Cyders et al., 2014; Lynam, 2013) was used to measure negative urgency (i.e., a tendency to act rashly as a result of negative affect), positive urgency (i.e., a tendency to act rashly as a result of positive affect), sensation seeking (i.e., a tendency to seek novel or exciting experiences), (lack of) perseverance (i.e., an inability to stay focused on a task), and (lack of) premeditation (i.e., a tendency to act without thinking). It consists of twenty items with responses ranging from 1 (agree strongly) to 4 (disagree strongly), with four items used to assess each of the five traits of impulsivity. Responses were coded so that higher scores indicate higher levels of trait impulsivity. Reported scores represent the total score for each scale. The SUPPS-P was adapted from the 59-item, UPPS-P (Lynam, Smith, Whiteside, & Cyders, 2006). SUPPS-P sub-scale scores have shown to be similar to UPPS-P sub-scales (Cyders et al., 2014).

Careless Responding

Careless responding was assessed by the use of four "bogus items" placed throughout the test ("I have never brushed my teeth," "I do not understand a word of English," "I sleep less than one hour per night," and "I have been to every country in the world"), Participants responded to items on a 1 (agree strongly) to 7 (disagree strongly) scale. Any participant responding with a 1 or 2 on careless responding items had their data removed from analysis, as determined *a priori* (Meade & Craig, 2012).

Procedure

Data for the current study was part of a larger study posted on Amazon's MTurk as "E-cigarette, cigarette, and alcohol use survey." Workers who signed up to complete the study were given access to the Survey Monkey URL for the study. Participants were next asked if they consume alcohol and if they were over 21, and answering no to either item resulted in disqualification. After meeting study requirements participants responded to the above-described questionnaires (and other questionnaires not examined in the current study) and were given a survey code. All workers that provided a survey code were compensated 75 cents. Participants that completed the study at two time-points were matched based on their MTurk worker ID and survey code.

RESULTS

Preliminary Data Cleaning and Characteristics

Less than 0.01% of data was missing at random; therefore, missing data was imputed using linear interpolation. All scales were approximately normally distributed (skewness ranged -0.01 to 1.05, kurtosis ranged from -2.0 to 2.60). Table 1 presents mean values on study variables and comparisons across gender. The average AUDIT score was 6.63 (SD = 4.95), and the average number of total drinks over two weeks was 14.38 (SD = 14.93). Negative urgency scores had a mean of 8.60 (SD = 2.62), positive urgency scores had a mean of 6.98 (SD = 2.55), sensation seeking scores had a mean of 9.57 (SD = 2.94), lack of perseverance scores had a mean of 6.74 (SD = 1.99), and lack of premeditation scores had a mean of 6.58 (SD = 2.03).

Men reported significantly higher scores on AUDIT, $t(1289) = 3.18$, $p = .002$, total drinks, $t(1289) = 3.25$, $p = .001$, negative urgency, $t(1289) = 2.44$, $p = .02$, positive urgency, $t(1289) = 7.29$, $p < .001$, sensation seeking, $t(1289) = 11.59$, $p < .001$, and lack of perseverance, $t(1289) = 2.88$, $p = .004$, than women. Additionally, younger age was significantly associated with higher AUDIT ($r = -0.12$, $p < .001$), negative urgency ($r = -0.24$, $p < .001$), positive urgency ($r = -0.24$, $p < .001$), and sensation seeking ($r = -0.21$, $p < .001$).

Table 1. SUPPS-P, AUDIT and total drinks descriptive statistics and differences by gender

	Mean	*SD*	Min	Max	Male Mean (*SD*)	Female Mean (*SD*)	Independent t-test between genders	Relationship with Age (Pearson's *r*)
AUDIT	6.63	4.95	0	34	7.07 (5.07)	6.20 (4.80)	3.18*	-.12**
Total Drinks	14.38	14.93	0	57	15.75 (12.73)	13.05 (13.89)	3.25**	-.04
Negative Urgency	8.60	2.62	4	16	8.78 (2.49)	8.42 (2.74)	2.44*	-.24**
Positive Urgency	6.98	2.55	4	16	7.49 (2.55)	6.47 (2.44)	7.29**	-.24**
Sensation Seeking	9.57	2.94	4	16	10.47 (2.80)	8.66 (2.80)	11.59**	-.21**
Lack of Perseverance	6.74	1.99	4	16	6.90 (2.08)	6.66 (1.86)	2.88*	-.05
Lack of Premeditation	6.58	2.03	4	14	6.61 (2.02)	6.56 (2.04)	0.49	-.04

Note: Mean and SD for study variables by gender. Independent samples t-test were conducted to test differences between gender. Pearson's r was calculated between age and study variables. $^{*}p < .05$, $^{**}p < .001$.

Internal Consistency

Internal consistency estimates were good in the current sample: AUDIT responses (α = 0.80), negative urgency (α = .79), lack of perseverance (α = 0.72), lack of premeditation (α = 0.80), sensation seeking (α = 0.72), and positive urgency (α = 0.77).

Content Validity via Confirmatory Factor Analysis

We conducted two competing models using confirmatory factor analysis via the lavaan package in R3.0.1 (Beaujean, 2013). We fixed the scale by setting the variance of each latent variable to itself equal to 1. Because each item used a Likert scale, each item was treated as an ordinal variable. To assess the degree of fit, we used the following indices with fit recommendations in parentheses as suggested by Hu and Bentler (1998): $\chi2$ ($p > 0.05$); Root Mean Square Error of Approximation (RMSEA < 0.10); Tucker Lewis Index (TLI > 0.95); and Comparative Fit Index (CFI > 0.95).

Model 1 (as supported by Cyders et al., 2014) denoted a five factor model in which the items were distributed as follows: lack of perseverance (LPS) factor with items 1, 4, 7, and 11; the lack of premeditation (LPL) factor with items 2, 5, 12, and 19; the sensation seeking (SS) factor with items 9, 14, 16, and 18; the negative urgency (NUR) factor with items 6, 8, 13, and 15; and the positive urgency (PUR) factor with items 3, 10, 17, and 20. Fit indices for the model were: $\chi2 = 37856.18$, $p < 0.01$, $df = 190$; RMSEA = 0.06, 90% *CI* = 0.05-0.06; TLI = 0.98; CFI = 0.98. This model met criteria in all indices except for a significant $\chi2$ *p*-value, which is very difficult to obtain with a large sample size (Kline, 1998).

Although Model 1 had acceptable fit, we wanted to compare it to the fit of alternative model to assure best fit (also as done by Cyders et al., 2014). Model 2 was a single-factor model in which all items were distributed onto one factor. The fit indices for Model 2 were: $\chi2 = 7985.71$, $p < 0.01$, $df = 170$; RMSEA = 0.19, 90% *CI* = 0.19-0.20; TLI = 0.77; CFI = 0.79. No fit indices for Model 2 meet criteria for good fit, suggesting Model 1 is the better fitting model for the data.

Convergent and Divergent Validity Support

AUDIT, total drinks and SUPPS-P scale scores were significantly correlated (all p's < .05), with the exceptions of the relationships between AUDIT and lack of perseverance, total drinks and negative urgency, total drinks and lack of perseverance, and total drinks and lack of premeditation (see Table 2). As expected, SUPPS-P scales were significantly positively correlated, with the exception of the sensation seeking scale with lack of perseverance and lack of premeditation.

SUPPS-P subscales were grouped into three sets (see Cyders & Smith, 2007) to examine their relationship with AUDIT scores: 1) urgency (negative and positive urgency), 2) sensation seeking, and 3) lack of conscientiousness (lack of perseverance and lack of premeditation). Hierarchical linear regression was conducted in the following steps: 1) age, gender (0-male, 1-female), ethnicity (reference group - Caucasian), 2) lack of conscientiousness traits (lack of perseverance and lack of premeditation), 3) sensation seeking, and 4) urgency traits (negative and positive urgency). Urgency traits were significantly related to AUDIT scores ($\Delta R^2 = 0.02$, $p < .001$) above and beyond demographics ($\Delta R^2 = 0.03$, $p < .001$), sensation seeking ($\Delta R^2 = 0.002$, $p = .11$), and lack of conscientiousness traits ($\Delta R^2 = 0.02$, $p < .001$; see Table 3).

DISCUSSION

Overall, the data gathered from the present MTurk samples show adequate reliability and validity, supporting the use of MTurk data in alcohol and social science research. As hypothesized, the reliability analyses showed adequate internal consistency of the data for AUDIT and SUPPS-P subscales, similar to estimates found in previous work (e.g., Lynam et al., 2006; Murphy & MacKillop, 2012; Whiteside & Lynam, 2001; Zapolski, Cyders, & Smith, 2009).

Table 2. Pearson's *r* correlations between SUPPS-P sub-scales, AUDIT, and Total Drinks

	AUDIT	Negative Urgency	Positive Urgency	Sensation Seeking	Lack of Perseverance	Lack of Premed-itation
Negative Urgency	.17**					
Positive Urgency	.20**	.64**				
Sensation Seeking	.10**	.36**	.35**			
Lack of Perseverance	.04	.14**	.18**	-.09*		
Lack of Premeditation	.14**	.36**	.39**	.08*	.54**	
Total Drinks	.65**	.05	.08*	.09*	-.05	.02

* $p < .05$, ** $p < .001$.

Table 3. Hierarchical linear regression with SUPPS-P as related to AUDIT scores

DV: AUDIT	Beta	*t*	*p*	95% CI lower bound	95% CI upper bound	ΔR^2	*F*	*p*
Step 1						0.03	7.44	*<.001*
Gender	-0.07	-2.40	0.02	-1.26	-0.13			
How many years old	-0.07	-2.45	0.01	-0.06	-0.01			
AfAm	0.10	3.75	0.00	1.02	3.25			
Hisp	0.02	0.63	0.53	-0.74	1.43			
Other	-0.01	-0.41	0.68	-2.52	1.64			
Asian	-0.04	-1.64	0.10	-2.55	0.23			
Step 2						0.02	13.24	*<.001*
Lack of Premeditation	0.10	2.76	*0.01*	0.07	0.40			
Lack of Perseverance	-0.04	-1.14	0.25	-0.25	0.07			
Step 3						0.002	2.55	.11
Sensation Seeking	0.00	0.15	0.88	-0.10	0.11			
Step 4						0.02	9.12	*<.001*
Negative Urgency	0.06	1.51	0.13	-0.03	0.24			
Positive Urgency	0.10	2.68	*0.01*	0.05	0.34			

Note: Hierarchical linear regression, controlling for age, gender (male-0, female-1), and ethnicity (Caucasian-reference group), between SUPPS-P 3 factor structure scales and AUDIT scores. Bolded values indicate significant p-values at the $p < .05$ level.

The present study also provided adequate support for content, convergent and divergent validity of data collected from this MTurk sample. The confirmatory factor analysis upheld the superiority of a five-factor structure of the SUPPS-P as compared to the single-factor structure, consistent with previous work using the SUPPS-P (Cyders et al., 2014). The SUPPS-P scales were related to each other as expected: all scales were significantly positively correlated with each other with the exception to the relationships between sensation seeking with lack of perseverance and lack of premeditation (as supported by other work; e.g., Cyders et al., 2014). In line with previous literature, AUDIT, total drinks (measured by TLFB) and SUPPS-P were significantly related (Amlung et al., 2013; Cyders et al., 2014; Murphy & MacKillop, 2012). Importantly, the current data replicate previous findings, showing that positive and negative urgency are related to problematic alcohol consumption over and above demographics and the other SUPPS-P traits. This replicates previous work highlighting the unique role of urgency in problematic alcohol consumption (e.g., Coskunpinar et al., 2013).

Using commonly used measures in alcohol research, our findings provide evidence for the reliability and validity of data collected from MTurk samples, and support the viability of using this popular but emerging approach to data collection. The demographics of our MTurk samples are similar to previously reported MTurk demographics and more closely align with demographics of the U.S population than college student samples. Problematic alcohol use is a serious public health concern that affects various age groups, but alcohol research often samples college students due to convenience and low cost (NIAAA, 2015; Peterson, 2001). To this end, our study suggests that data collection using MTurk sample can be a more representative alternative allowing faster data collection and producing empirical findings that are more generalizable to the US population, while maintaining robust psychometric properties.

There are some limitations in the current study. First, the present MTurk sample is largely comprised of Caucasians, which questions the generalizability of findings to other racial/ethnic population. Despite this limitation, the present samples resemble the current demographics in the United States (Caucasian = 77.4%; US Census Bureau, 2015). Second, the participants self-selected the study, which was titled as "E-cigarette, cigarette, and alcohol use survey." Individuals who use electronic cigarettes, cigarettes and alcohol might have been more likely to complete the survey, which could bias study findings. However, these characteristics of present MTurk samples resemble samples often found in alcohol research as smoking status is related to alcohol use (e.g., McKee, Falba, O'Malley, Sindelar, & O'Connor, 2007). Third, findings could be limited by self-report biases related to self-report data collection methods.

In conclusion, the current study provides supportive evidence for psychometric properties of data gathered from MTurk samples. Although some remaining limitations remain concerning self-report biases, our results suggest viability of using MTurk for alcohol and social science research (Buhrmester et al., 2011; Shapiro et al., 2013). In particular, MTurk can provide data that is more representative of the US population than data collected from college student samples, making it a good tool for scale development and for examining theories that better generalize to a non-college student population.

References

Amlung, M., Few, L. R., Howland, J., Rohsenow, D. J., Metrik, J., and MacKillop, J. (2013). Impulsivity and alcohol demand in relation to combined alcohol and caffeine use. *Experimental and Clinical Psychopharmacology*, 21(6), 467–74. http://doi.org/10.1037/a0034214.

Andover, M. S. (2014). Non-suicidal self-injury disorder in a community sample of adults. *Psychiatry Research*, 219(2), 305–310. http://doi.org/10.1016/j.psychres.2014.06.001.

Beaujean, A. A. (2013). Factor Analysis using R. *Practical Assessment, Research and Evaluation*, 18(4), 1–11. Retrieved from http://pareonline.net/pdf/v18n4.pdf.

Berinsky, A. J., Huber, G. A., and Lenz, G. S. (2012). Evaluating Online Labor Markets for Experimental Research: Amazon.com's Mechanical Turk. *Political Analysis*, 20(3), 351–368. http://doi.org/10.1093/pan/mpr057.

Boynton, M. H., and Richman, L. S. (2014). An online daily diary study of alcohol use using Amazon's mechanical turk. *Drug and Alcohol Review*, 33(4), 456–461. http://doi.org/10.1111/dar.12163.

Buhrmester, M., Kwang, T., and Gosling, S. D. (2011). Amazon's Mechanical Turk: A New Source of Inexpensive, Yet High-Quality, Data? *Perspectives on Psychological Science*, 6(1), 3–5. http://doi.org/10.1177/1745691610393980.

Coskunpinar, A., Dir, A. L., and Cyders, M. a. (2013). Multidimensionality in Impulsivity and Alcohol Use: A Meta-Analysis Using the UPPS Model of Impulsivity. *Alcoholism: Clinical and Experimental Research*, 37(9), 1441–1450. http://doi.org/10.1111/acer.12131.

Cyders, M. A., Littlefield, A. K., Coffey, S., and Karyadi, K. A. (2014). Examination of a short English version of the UPPS-P Impulsive Behavior Scale. *Addictive Behaviors*, 39(9), 1372–1376. http://doi.org/10.1016/j.addbeh.2014.02.013.

Cyders, M. A., and Smith, G. T. (2007). Mood-based rash action and its components: positive and negative urgency. *Personality and Individual Differences*, 43, 839–850.

Donovan, D. M., Kivlahan, D. R., Doyle, S. R., Longabaugh, R., and Greenfield, S. F. (2006). Concurrent validity of the Alcohol Use Disorders Identification Test (AUDIT) and AUDIT zones in defining levels of severity among out-patients with alcohol dependence in the COMBINE study. *Addiction*, 101(12), 1696–1704. http://doi.org/10.1111/j.1360-0443.2006.01606.x.

Farrell, N. R., Lee, A. A., and Deacon, B. J. (2015). Biological or psychological? Effects of eating disorder psychoeducation on self-blame and recovery expectations among symptomatic individuals. *Behaviour Research and Therapy*, 74(October), 32–37. http://doi.org/10.1016/j.brat.2015.08.011.

Fergus, T. A., and Bardeen, J. R. (2014). Emotion regulation and obsessive–compulsive symptoms: A further examination of associations. *Journal of Obsessive-Compulsive and Related Disorders*, 3(3), 243–248. http://doi.org/10.1016/j.jocrd.2014.06.001.

Gardner, R. M., Brown, D. L., and Boice, R. (2012). Using Amazon's Mechanical Turk website to measure accuracy of body size estimation and body dissatisfaction. *Body Image*, 9(4), 532–534. http://doi.org/10.1016/j.bodyim.2012.06.006.

Goodman, J. K., Cryder, C. E., and Cheema, A. (2013). Data Collection in a Flat World: The Strengths and Weaknesses of Mechanical Turk Samples. *Journal of Behavioral Decision Making*, 26(3), 213–224. http://doi.org/10.1002/bdm.1753.

Guth, S., Lindberg, S. A., Badger, G. J., Thomas, C. S., Rose, G. L., and Helzer, J. E. (2008). Brief Intervention in Alcohol-Dependent Versus Nondependent Individuals. *Journal of Studies on Alcohol and Drugs*, 69 (2), 243–250.

Hallford, D. J., and Mellor, D. (2016). Autobiographical Memory and Depression : Identity-continuity and Problem-solving Functions Indirectly Predict Symptoms over Time through Psychological Well-being. *Applied Cognitivie Psychology*, 30(2), 152-159. doi: 10.1002/acp.3169.

Hershberger, A. R., Karyadi, K. A., VanderVeen, J. D., and Cyders, M. A. (2016). Combined expectancies of alcohol and e-cigarette use relate to higher alcohol use. *Addictive Behaviors*, 52, 13–21. http://doi.org/10.1016/j.addbeh.2015.08.005.

Hoeppner, B. B., Stout, R. L., Jackson, K. M., and Barnett, N. P. (2010). How good is fine-grained Timeline Follow-back data? Comparing 30-day TLFB and repeated 7-day TLFB alcohol consumption reports on the person and daily level. *Addictive Behaviors*, 35(12), 1138–1143. http://doi.org/10.1016/j.addbeh.2010.08.013.

Hu, L., and Bentler, P. M. (1998). Fit indices in covariance structure modeling: Sensitivity to underparameterized model misspecification. *Psychological Methods*, 3(4), 424–453. Retrieved from http://psycnet.apa.org/journals/met/3/4/424/.

Kline, R. B. (1998). *Principles and Practice of Structural Equation Modeling*. NY: The Guilford Press.

Lac, A., and Berger, D. E. (2013). Development and validation of the Alcohol Myopia Scale. *Psychological Assessment*, 25(3), 738–747. http://doi.org/10.1037/a0032535.

Lovett, D. E., Ham, L. S., and Veilleux, J. C. (2015). Psychometric evaluation of a standardized set of alcohol cue photographs to assess craving. *Addictive Behaviors*, 48, 58–61. http://doi.org/10.1016/j.addbeh.2015.05.002.

Lynam, D. R. (2013). Development of a short form of the UPPS-P Impulsive Behavior Scale. *Unpublished Technical Report.*

Lynam, D. R., Smith, G. T., Whiteside, S. P., and Cyders, M. A. (2006). *The UPPS-P: Asessing five personality pathways to impulsive behavior*. West Lafayette, IN.: Purdue University.

McKee, S. A., Falba, T., O'Malley, S. S., Sindelar, J., and O'Connor, P. G. (2007). Smoking status as a clinical indicator for alcohol misuse in US adults. *Archives of Internal Medicine*, 167(7), 716–721. http://doi.org/10.1001/archinte.167.7.716.

Meade, A. W., and Craig, S. B. (2012). Identifying careless responses in survey data. *Psychological Methods*, 17(3), 437–455. http://doi.org/10.1037/a0028085.

Murphy, C., and MacKillop, J. (2012). Living in the here and now: Interrelationships between impulsivity, mindfulness, and alcohol misuse. *Psychopharmacology*, 219(2). http://doi.org/10.1007/s00213-011-2573-0.

Paolacci, G., and Chandler, J. (2014). Inside the Turk: Understanding Mechanical Turk as a Participant Pool. *Current Directions in Psychological Science*, 23(3), 184–188. http://doi.org/10.1177/0963721414531598.

Paolacci, G., Chandler, J., and Ipeirotis, P. G. (2010). Running experiments on amazon mechanical turk. *Judgment and Decision Making*, 5(5), 411–419. http://doi.org/10.2139/ssrn.1626226.

Peterson, R. A. (2001). On the Use of College Students in Social Science Research: Insights from a Second-Order Meta-analysis. *Journal of Consumer Research*, 28(3), 450–461. http://doi.org/10.1086/323732.

Rueger, S. Y., Trela, C. J., Palmeri, M., and King, A. C. (2012). Self-administered web-based timeline followback procedure for drinking and smoking behaviors in young adults. *Journal of Studies on Alcohol and Drugs*, 73(5), 829–833.

Saunders, J. B., Aasland, O. G., Babor, T. F., de la Fuente, J. R., and Grant, M. (1993). Development of the Alcohol Use Disorders Identification Test (AUDIT): WHO Collaborative Project on Early Detection of Persons with Harmful Alcohol Consumption--II. *Addiction*, 88, 791–804. http://doi.org/10.1111/j.1360-0443.1993.tb02093.x.

Shapiro, D. N., Chandler, J., and Mueller, P. A. (2013). Using Mechanical Turk to study clinical populations. *Clinical Psychological Science*, 1(2), 213–220. http://doi.org/10.1177/2167702612469015.

Shields, A. L., and Caruso, J. C. (2003). Reliability generalization of the alcohol use disorders identification test. *Educational and Psychological Measurement*, 63(3), 404–413. http://doi.org/10.1177/0013164403251327.

Sobell, L. C., and Sobell, M. B. (1992). Timeline Follow-back: A technique for assessing self-reported ehtanol consumption. In: J. Allen and R. Z. Litten (Eds.), *Measuring Alcohol Consumption: Psychosocial and biological methods* (pp. 41–72). Totowa, NJ: Humana Press.

VanderBroek, L., Acker, J., Palmer, A. A., de Wit, H., and MacKillop, J. (2015). Interrelationships among parental family history of substance misuse, delay discounting, and personal substance use. *Psychopharmacology*. http://doi.org/10.1007/s00213-015-4074-z.

Whiteside, S. P., and Lynam, D. R. (2001). The five factor model and impulsivity: Using a structural model of personality to understand impulsivity. *Personality and Individual Differences*, 30(4), 669–689. http://doi.org/10.1016/S0191-8869(00)00064-7.

Wymbs, B. T., and Dawson, A. E. (2015). Screening Amazon's Mechanical Turk for Adults With ADHD. *Journal of Attention Disorders*, 1–10. http://doi.org/10.1177/1087054715597471.

Zapolski, T. C. B., Cyders, M. A., and Smith, G. T. (2009). Positive urgency predicts illegal drug use and risky sexual behavior. *Psychology of Addictive Behaviors*, 23(2), 348–354. http://doi.org/10.1037/a0014684.

In: Substance Abuse
Editor: Tanya Reid

ISBN: 978-1-63485-612-6

Chapter 3

Improvement in Attitudes towards Sexuality Regarding Treated Patients with Alcohol Dependence Syndrome

Aleš Friedl*

Psihiatrična bolnišnica Ormož, Ormož,
Ormož, Slovenia

Abstract

Background: Alcohol dependence syndrome is related to sexual difficulties, e.g., a decrease or a loss of libido, erectile dysfunction, premature ejaculation and a decreased libido. This study was undertaken to assess and compare certain parameters of sexual functioning in patients with alcohol dependence syndrome.

Subjects and methods: The study population consisted of 106 patients diagnosed with the alcohol dependency syndrome between 26 and 71 years of age who were treated and followed in Psychiatric Hospital Ormož between 2010 and 2012. The patients were followed in hospital and post-hospital setting. An abbreviated version of the Eysenck's Inventory of attitudes to sex was used in this study.

* Corresponding author: e-mail: alfr777@gmail.com, tel.: +386 2 7415 110, fax: + 386 2 7415 147.

Results: In the aspect of the libido and pornography there is a significant statistical difference in the field of gender, i.e., men compared to women have an increased libido. In regard to the factor "sexual satisfaction" the post-hospital group shows a greater presence of this factor than the hospital group. As by the libido, regarding the sexual satisfaction there are as well no significant differences among the depressed and the non-depressed patients with the alcohol dependency syndrome – a probable reason lies in the use of antidepressant drugs.

Conclusion: In the post-hospital group of patients the improvement in attitudes towards the sexuality occurs spontaneously without any specific targeted therapeutic treatment.

Keywords: sexuality, alcoholics, libido, sexual satisfaction, Eysenck

INTRODUCTION

1. Alcoholism and Sexuality

In 1964 a WHO Expert Committee introduced the term "dependence" to replace the terms "addiction" and "habituation" (Dependence syndrome 2014). The Tenth Revision of the International Classification of Diseases and Health Problems (ICD-10) defines the dependence syndrome as being a cluster of physiological, behavioural, and cognitive phenomena in which the use of a substance or a class of substances takes on a much higher priority for a given individual than other behaviour that once had greater value. Central descriptive characteristics of the dependence syndrome are desire (often strong, sometimes overpowering), use of the psychoactive drugs (which may have been medically prescribed or not), alcohol, or tobacco (The ICD-10, 1994).

While DSM-IV-TR still defines a distinction between alcohol abuse and alcohol dependence, DSM-V does not separate the diagnoses of substance abuse and dependence as in the DSM-IV-TR. The DSM-V puts at the forefront the severity of disorder, taking into account the number of symptoms. It classifies the alcohol use disorder into three categories: a mild alcohol use disorder is suggested by the presence of two to three symptoms, a moderate one by four to five symptoms and a severe one, by six or more symptoms (DSM-V 2013). Compared to the DSM-IV-TR, the DSM-V lists all the criteria that have been classified either under the heading "alcohol abuse" or under the heading "alcohol dependence" with an exception of a category "Recurrent alcohol-related legal problems (e.g., arrests for alcohol- related disorderly conduct)," which can be found in the diagnostic criteria of "alcohol abuse" in the DSM-IV-TR. A novelty in the DSM-V is the category "Craving, or a strong desire or urge to use alcohol."

A quick glimpse of the criteria in the process of diagnosis of alcohol dependence according to the ICD-10, or alcohol use disorder according to the DSM-V, shows that problems in sex life are not one of the criteria for this disorder, although many alcoholics have such problems (probably more than average people). The Big Book of Alcoholics Anonymous says: "We all have sex problems and we'd hardly be human if we didn't" (Anonymous 2013). The closer look at the criteria according to the ICD-10 and the DSM-V shows that sexual disturbances are included in the process of diagnosis of alcohol dependence or alcohol use disorder. In the ICD-10 there is a statement: "Progressive neglect of alternative pleasures or interests because of psychoactive substance use" (Dependence syndrome 2014) and in the DSM-V there is a statement: "Important social, occupational, or recreational activities may be given up or reduced because of substance use (Criterion 7)" (DSM-V 2013).

Sexual dysfunctions can occur in association with intoxication or with withdrawal of alcohol (DSM-V 2013).

The alcoholics of both sexes have sexual difficulties. Males have a decrease or a loss of libido, erectile dysfunction and premature ejaculation (Vijayasenan 1981; Jensen 1984; Miller Gold 1988; Mack, Harrington, Frances 2010). Also women have a decreased libido (Heiser, Hartmann 1987; Seki, Yoshida, Okamura 1991). Excessive alcohol consumption leads to lower satisfaction with sexuality (Miller, Gold 1988; Roman 1988). On the other hand, there are records that identify the contrary, namely that alcohol increases the libido (Shakespeare 1606/2014; Abel 1980; Beckman, Ackerman 1995; Leigh, Stall 1993; Bjekić, Vlajinac, Marinkovic 1999; Cooper 2002; Farris, Treat, Viken 2010; Gilmore et al. 2013). Lynne Cooper notes that drinking can promote, inhibit, or have no effect on behaviour, depending on the interplay of factors governing the behaviour and a particular situation and the content of individually held beliefs about alcohol's effects (Cooper 2010).

2. Depression and Sexuality

In comparison with alcoholism the area of sexuality characterizes one of the conditions for the diagnosis of depression. This area is on one hand defined indirectly, as a "loss of interests or pleasure" in the ICD-10 (Gpnotebook 2014; Bluebook 2014), and on the other hand quite directly as "a marked loss of libido" (Bluebook 2014), wherein a depressive person has to meet at least four symptoms of depression (Gpnotebook 2014).

Similarly, in the DSM-V a scope of sex, regarding to Major Depressive Episode, is expressed indirectly as "markedly diminished interest or pleasure in all, or almost all, activities most of the day, nearly every day (as indicated by either subjective account or observation) ," and on the other hand directly: "In some individuals, there is a significant reduction from previous levels of sexual interest or desire" (DSM-V 2013).

Experts estimate that about 70 percent of people with depression will experience the sexual dysfunction. Men may experience erectile dysfunction (impotence), a decline in sexual desire and difficulties with ejaculation. Among men, the rate of sexual dysfunction is estimated to be 23-50 percent (Kiefer 2015). Among depressed women, the rate of sexual dysfunction is estimated to be as high as 33-90 percent. The depression related to sexual dysfunction among women usually takes the form of difficulties with becoming aroused (such as uncomfortable vaginal dryness), and an inability to achieve orgasm or delayed orgasm (Kiefer 2015).

On the other hand, antidepressants can cause sexual dysfunction. Antidepressant medicines are highly effective in helping to ease the depression. However, many of these drugs have undesirable side effects, including sexual problems as a consequence. Some antidepressants may make it difficult for a man to have an erection. For both men and women, sexual problems can mean being unable to initiate, participate fully in, or enjoy sex. Such complications can lead to a loss of self-confidence that can, in turn, undermine a depression recovery. In addition, side effects tend to increase with higher doses of antidepressants (The Cleveland Clinic Foundation 2015).

Regarding the relationship between sex and depression, it is necessary to know the following. Some depressed people manage to maintain normal sex lives – sometimes even finding that sex is the only thing that gives them comfort and reassurance (Webber 2015).

3. Depression and Alcoholism

The long-term alcohol consumption, despite the original intention to make an individual get rid of feelings of guilt and anxiety, often leads to anxiety and depression. Symptoms of depression and panic disorders may be present in terms of insomnia, lowered mood, agitation, chest pain, palpitations. Alcohol otherwise temporarily alleviate symptoms, but leads to a vicious circle of drinking and outbreak of symptoms (Kaplan, Sadock 1989).

Alcohol is a depressor of the central nervous system. A regular consumption of high doses of alcohol causes feelings of depression. Commonly, abstinence results in agitation and nervousness, including the anxiety. The more the person drinks, more likely these symptoms occur. The depressive symptoms are reported by 80% of alcoholics. Around 30% of men and 50% of women report protracted periods of severe depression. Approximately 20% of alcoholics attempt to commit suicide (once or repeatedly) and approximately 15% of them die by committing suicide. The diagnosis can only be used in cases where symptoms clinically significantly impair the social, labour or other functioning (Gelder, López-Ibor, Andreasen 2004).

Excessive alcohol intake over several days results in many symptoms of severe depressive episode (without psychotic symptoms). The improvement comes within a few days to 4 weeks after the establishment of abstinence. 80% of alcoholics report periods of intense depression, but only 5% of men and 10% of women have the severe depressive episode (without psychotic symptoms) when they do not get drunk excessively (Kaplan, Sadock 1989).

For most alcoholics the severe depressive episode is usually quickly resolved without a medical therapy (Kaplan, Sadock 1989; Gelder, López-Ibor, Andreasen 2004).

The decreased libido or reduced sexual satisfaction by alcoholics is not necessarily solely the result of the alcohol consumption, but also the depression. Alcoholic populations display significantly more depression, paranoid thinking trends, aggressive feelings and acts, and significantly lower self-esteem, responsibility and self-control than non-alcoholic populations (Selzer 1980). However, the work done by many researchers suggests that despite what alcoholics tell us, objective observation in the laboratory reveals that chronic use of alcohol makes alcoholic subjects more withdrawn, less self-confident, often more anxious, and commonly more depressed with increased suicidal ideation (McNamee, Mendelson, Mello 1968; Tamerin, Weiner, Mendelson 1970; Nathan et al., 1970; Allman, Taylor, Nathan 1972; Logue et al. 1978).

On the other hand, alcoholism can mask the depression. The mood change may also be masked by added features such as irritability, excessive consumption of alcohol, histrionic behaviour, and exacerbation of pre-existing phobic or obsessional symptoms, or by hypochondriac preoccupations (Bluebook 2014).

Many alcoholics get depressed in an initial period of abstinence. Data show that about a quarter of people recovering from alcoholism experience the anxiety and the depression, which can persist up to 2 years (Janicak et al. 2011). In this respect they have a lower libido (Graziottin 1998; Kobayashi et al. 1999). When the abstinence is prolonged, however, they regain a normal sexual functioning (Mack, Harrington, Frances 2010).

4. Treatment of Alcoholism in Slovenia

In Slovenia the treatment may be roughly divided into three stages:

- a preparatory phase,
- a level of intensive care,
- rehabilitation.

In the preparatory phase a patient is deployed in a psychiatric clinic where a psychiatrist performs an ambulatory inspection and, if necessary, refers the person to check in at a clinical psychologist. The intensive treatment takes place in a mental institution or a psychiatric hospital. The duration period in the hospital lasts about 3 months. The second phase is followed by the third phase, which means the inclusion of the patients in the "club for recovering alcoholics" (in which their family members are also included) or the inclusion in Alcoholics Anonymous (AA).

The goal of the therapy is to change the behaviour, and that means not only sobriety, but also the improvement in interpersonal relationships in the families, at work and in a broader society. The patients, who complete the treatment, mostly return to the same environment in which they previously dealt with excessive alcohol consumption, so it is important that after the treatment the person is able to solve everyday problems without alcohol. Modern methods of treatment allow a shift from an inpatient to an outpatient care, but the hospital care is often necessary, especially for people who cannot establish the abstinence in their environment, who have the severe abstinence symptoms, mental illness or other medical complications or who live in difficult social circumstances with a weak support in their environment (Židanik, Čebašek-Travnik 2003).

In the groups at the hospital and in the club for recovering alcoholics, the patients and the family members discuss various topics. The relatives and the alcoholics involved in a course of treatment often report the improvement of their interpersonal relations and the improvement in communication within families. They also report that now the patients carry out more work at home than before and they feel well while doing so. The work also strengthens their self-esteem and self-confidence.

After completing the hospital treatment and integration into the clubs for recovering alcoholics, the patients who have completed the treatment in the Psychiatric Hospital Ormož have the option to attend the post-hospital group once a month for one year. Questions about sexuality are sometimes cleared in both hospital and post-hospital groups.

5. The Purpose of the Study

The purpose of the study is to discover whether there are differences in the attitudes towards sexuality in relation to the libido and sexual satisfaction among the hospital and the post-hospital patient population, while taking into account the factor of depression, which may lower the attitudes towards sexuality.

Subjects and Methods

Participants

In the study participated 106 patients diagnosed with the alcohol dependency syndrome, who were treated in the Psychiatric Hospital Ormož. 48 patients were hospitalized and 58 of them were in the post-hospital group. The patients in the post-hospital group attended the group meeting once a month after they had been treated at the Psychiatric Hospital Ormož. The questionnaires were fulfilled anonymously. The patients entered only their age, gender and whether they have a partner or not. Sometimes the patients did not mark their gender. For this reason, the sample where it was possible to determine the gender of the respondents is lesser than the total sample. In the sample of the hospitalized patients, 38 were men (95%) and 2 were women (5%), in the sample of the post-hospital patients, 41 were men (77%) and 12 were women (23%). On the basis of data on age and sex, patients with depression were identified retrospectively. Since the groups were relatively small (7 to 12 persons, with the exception of one group of 20 persons), this was in many cases possible, but not always. The identification was not possible when there were 2 or 3 patients of the same age and the same gender in the group. For this reason, the number of the identified patients with depression or without depression is lower than the overall sample.

In the group of the hospitalized patients there were 25 (52%) depressive patients and in the post-hospital group 26 (44%) of them. The diagnosis of the alcohol dependence syndrome and the depression assessment was conducted by a psychiatrist, who also introduced the antidepressant therapy. The number of patients with a partner was 27 (56%) in the hospital group and 36 (62%) in the post-hospital group.

Measures

An abbreviated version of the Eysenck's Inventory of attitudes to sex (Eysenck 1976) was used in this study. The original inventory has 158 items, while the abbreviated inventory has 52 (Lamovec 1980). The abbreviated inventory includes only those items that have made a similar correlation in both sexes and a saturation of one of the two super factors (sexual libido and sexual satisfaction) exceeding 0.30 (Lamovec 1980).

Procedures

The patients were given instructions: "Carefully read each statement and then circle the answer "YES" or "NO," depending on your point of view. If you cannot decide, circle "?." Answer all questions. There are no right or wrong answers. Do not hesitate too long, but try to answer according to your feelings immediately."

In order to avoid potential embarrassment of the patients in solving the questionnaire and to increase the provision of a sense of anonymity - regardless the fact that the groups were small - the researcher left the room with an instruction that the last one brings him all completed questionnaires.

The samples of the patients were not random. The questionnaires were fulfilled by the patients who were in the group at given time.

A statistical analysis of the results was performed with the software SPSS for Windows 21.0.

RESULTS

A. Sexual Libido

According to Eysenck the super factor "sexual libido" refers to items such as: "Great Strength of sexual desire," "Get sexually excited easily," "Get a pleasant feeling from touching my sexual parts," "Thinking about sex almost every day," "Preference for having intercourse frequently," "Being involved in more than one sex affair at time" (Eysenck 1976).

1. In the aspect of the libido there is no significant difference between the hospital and the post-hospital group, although the average of the hospital group is slightly lower than the average of the post-hospital group (44.75 against 48.34).
2. Differences in the libido were also not relevant among the group of the depressed patients and the group of the non-depressed patients, although the non-depressed patients demonstrated a slightly higher libido (49.84 against 43.75).
3. A significant difference in the libido does not appear even among the patients with partners and the patients without a partner, although the patients with a partner show a slightly higher level of libido (48.62 against 43.66).
4. A significant difference in the libido does not appear even among younger (of age 35 and younger) and senior patients (of age 36 and older). In average the younger ones have even lower libido than the older patients (47.38 against 56.31).
5. In the aspect of the libido there is a significant statistical difference only in the field of gender, i.e., men compared to women have an increased libido (49.03 against 33.47), the difference that was significant at the level of p = 000.
6. In relation to pornography there are significant differences among males and females in the sense that men are more inclined to the pornography than women (59.82 against 25.20). This difference is significant at the level of p = 000.

Table 1. The difference in libido among men and women tested by Independent Sample T-test

Group Statistics					
	Gender	N	Mean	Std. Deviation	Std. Error Mean
Libido	male	79	49,03	14,749	1,659
	female	15	33,47	12,415	3,205

Independent Samples Test										
		Levene's Test for Equality of Variances		t-test for Equality of Means						
		F	Sig.	t	Df	Sig. (2-tailed)	Mean Difference	Std. Error Difference	95% Confidence Interval of the Difference	
									Lower	Upper
Libido	Equal variances assumed	1,063	,305	3,831	92	,000	15,559	4,061	7,493	23,624
	Equal variances not assumed			4,310	22,223	,000	15,559	3,610	8,077	23,040

Table 2. The difference in relation to pornography among men and women tested by Independent Sample T-test

Group Statistics					
	Gender	N	Mean	Std. Deviation	Std. Error Mean
Pornography	male	79	59,82	31,466	3,540
	female	15	25,20	26,756	6,908

Independent Samples Test										
		Levene's Test for Equality of Variances		t-test for Equality of Means						
		F	Sig.	t	df	Sig. (2-tailed)	Mean Difference	Std. Error Difference	95% Confidence Interval of the Difference	
									Lower	Upper
Pornography	Equal variances assumed	2,619	,109	3,992	92	,000	34,623	8,674	17,396	51,849
	Equal variances not assumed			4,460	22,046	,000	34,623	7,763	18,526	50,720

B. Sexual Satisfaction

According to Eysenck the super factor "sexual satisfaction" refers to items such as: "Satisfied with sex life," "A partner satisfies all physical needs," "Feel sexually competent," "Not afraid of sexual relationships," "Easy to tell a partner likes/dislikes about love-making" (Eysenck 1976).

7. In regard to the super factor "sexual satisfaction" the post-hospital group shows a greater presence of this factor than the hospital group (61.09 against 44.33). The difference is significant at the p = 0.005 level.
8. As by the libido, regarding the sexual satisfaction there are as well no significant differences among the depressed and the non-depressed patients, even if the non-depressed patients express higher satisfaction (44.97 to 39.39).
9. In regard to the sexual satisfaction there exist statistically significant differences among the patients who have a partner and those who do not. The patients with a partner have a higher level of satisfaction (61.56 against 38.59). The difference is significant at the level of p = 000.

Table 3. The difference in satisfaction between the hospital and the post-hospital group tested with nonparametric Mann-Whitney U test

Ranks				
	Hospitalization	N	Mean Rank	Sum of Ranks
Satisfaction	hospital group	48	44,33	2128,00
	post-hospital group	58	61,09	3543,00
	Total	106		

Test Statistics[a]	
	Satisfaction
Mann-Whitney U	952,000
Wilcoxon W	2128,000
Z	-2,803
Asymp. Sig. (2-tailed)	,005

Table 4. The difference in satisfaction among the patients with a partner and the patients without a partner tested with nonparametric Mann-Whitney U test

Ranks				
	Partner Yes/No	N	Mean Rank	Sum of Ranks
Satisfaction	Yes	63	61,56	3878,00
	No	41	38,59	1582,00
	Total	104		

Test Statistics[a]	
	Satisfaction
Mann-Whitney U	721,000
Wilcoxon W	1582,000
Z	-3,809
Asymp. Sig. (2-tailed)	,000

10. Regarding the issue whether a partnership means prevention against depression, it should be noted that was not confirmed in our study, since the hospital and the post-hospital patients who are in the relationship and those who are not, have a similar percentage of the depression (62.50 vs. 60.00).

DISCUSSION

A. Sexual Libido

1. Regarding the libido there do not exist significant differences between the hospital and the post-hospital group, although the average of the hospital group is slightly lower than the average of the post-hospital group (44.75 against 48.34). This result is different than expected since the expectation was that the treatment of the alcoholism and the abstinence would increase the libido, although some treated alcoholics or their family members report a lower libido after they become sober (CAmom 2015; Mike 2008; Strauss, Turner, Dudek 1982).
2. The differences in the libido were not significant between the group of the depressed patients and the group of the non-depressed patients, although the non-depressed patients demonstrated a slightly higher libido (49.84 against 43.75). Such a result might be surprising, but it

should be known that the depressed patients received the antidepressant therapy, which is the factor that might reduce symptoms of depression including the side effect of the decreased libido. On the other hand, it is also true that not all people who suffer from the depression also have disorders in the area of sexuality (The Cleveland Clinic Foundation 2015).

3. There is no significant difference in the libido among the patients with partners and the patients without partners, although the patients with a partner show a slightly higher level of libido (48.62 against 43.66). In fact, it was expected that a higher level of libido would have the patients without a partner, because such an elevated libido would strengthen their efforts to find a partner.
4. There exist no significant differences in the libido among younger (of age 35 and younger) and senior (of age 36 and older) patients. The younger patients have even lower libido than the older patients (47.38 against 56.31). This result is even more surprising than the previous one, as opposed to the conclusion that with age a hormonal balance in elderly patients is destroyed and that lower secretion of testosterone would decline the libido. However, regardless the fact that there are differences between the two groups, this difference was not statistically significant.
5. Regarding the libido there is a significant difference only in the field of gender, i.e., men have an increased libido compared to women (49.03 against 33.47). The difference is significant at the level of $p = 000$. This result is consistent with the findings of Eysenck, who also got fully significant difference among men and women. Males achieved higher scores than females (Eysenck 1976). For this reason males are more quickly and easily sexually aroused than females and they more easily and more quickly reach an orgasm.
6. In relation to the pornography male and female alcoholics showed the significant difference in the sense that men are more inclined to the pornography than women (59.82 against 25.20). The difference is significant at the level of $p = 000$. The pornography is the factor that positively correlates with the libido (Eysenck 1976), and this applies also to the patients with the alcohol dependence syndrome.

B. Sexual Satisfaction

7. Sexual satisfaction in the post-hospital group is greater than in the hospital group (61.09 against 44.33). The difference was significant at the level p = 0.005. At first glance it seems that this result is surprising, since the hospital and the post-hospital group have no statistically significant differences in the libido. Common sense would expect that both the libido and the sexual satisfaction are interconnected. However, Eysenck (1976) found that these two factors are unrelated to each other, which is particularly true for men, where the correlation between the two is very low (r = 0:09), whereas by women, the correlation is somewhat greater (r = 00:31). The difference regarding the sexual satisfaction between the post-hospital and the hospital group may mean that the alcoholics who attend the post-hospital group may have a greater chance of abstinence than the alcoholics who do not decide to attend that kind of treatment.
8. As by the libido, regarding the sexual satisfaction there were as well no significant differences among the depressed and the non-depressed patients, although the satisfaction was by the non-depressed patients in average higher (44.97 to 39.39). As already mentioned, the depressed patients received the antidepressant therapy, which is the factor that might reduce the symptoms of depression, which as well include the reduced satisfaction. On the other hand, it is also true that people who suffer from depression do not show the symptoms in the area of sexuality (The Cleveland Clinic Foundation 2015).
9. In regard to the sexual satisfaction there exist statistically significant differences among patients who have a partner and those who do not. The patients with a partner have a higher level of satisfaction (61.56 against 38.59). The difference is significant at the level of p = 000. Given that sex is an area that offers the possibility of a human self-affirmation and it can also enhance self-esteem, the sexuality is one of the factors that contributes to the improvement of the individual's self-esteem and thereby discourages the consumption of alcohol. Many alcoholics consume alcoholic beverages because they do not appreciate themselves. A satisfactory partnership, which begins to be established during a course of the therapy, could in this respect represent the safeguard against relapse.

10. Regarding the issue whether the partnership is a kind of prevention against the depression, it should be noted that was not confirmed in this study, since the hospital and the post-hospital patients who are in the relationship and those who are not, have a similar percentage of the depression (62.5 % vs. 60.0%). There are numerous reasons for the occurrence of the depression. Some may be depressed because they do not have a partner, but would like to have one, while others are depressed because they have a partner, who they do not match with. However, the partnership as such is not the only factor for the occurrence of the depression. The contributing factors can also be unemployment, homelessness, loss of loved ones, organic mood disorder, etc.

Conclusion

In the post-hospital group of patients the improvement in attitudes towards the sexuality occurs spontaneously without any specific targeted therapeutic treatment. The patients are discharged from the hospital and once a week together with relatives they attend the group in the club for recovering alcoholics, and once a month they attend the group in the Psychiatric Hospital Ormož. Both, the patients and their relatives reported the improvement of their relations, better communication and the increased willingness to assist in work at home by the patient, which are all the factors that can be reflected in the area of sexuality.

References

Abel, E. L. (1980). A review of alcohol's effects on sex and reproduction. *Drug and Alcohol Dependence*, *5*(5), 321-332.

Allman, L. R., Taylor H. A. & Nathan, P. E. (1972). Group Drinking during Stress: Effects on Drinking Behavior, Affect, and Psychopathology. *American Journal of Psychiatry*, *129*(6), 669–678.

Anonymous, (2013). *Alcoholics Anonymous (Big Book)*, *4th edition*. New York: Alcoholics Anonymous World Services.

American Psychiatric Association (APA), (1994). *Diagnostic and Statistical Manual of Mental Disorders, 4th Edition*. Washington, DC: APA.

American Psychiatric Association (APA), (2000). *Diagnostic and Statistical Manual of Mental Disorders, 4th Edition, Text Revision*. Washington, DC: APA. retrieved from: http://www.ncbi.nlm.nih.gov/books/NBK44358/.

American Psychiatric Association (APA), (2013). *Diagnostic and Statistical Manual of Mental Disorders, 5th Edition*. Washington, DC: APA.

Beckman, L. J. & Ackerman, K. T. (1995). Women, alcohol, and sexuality. *Recent Developments in Alcoholism, 12*, 267-285.

Bjekić, M., Vlajinac, H. & Marinković, J. (1999). [Sociopathologic behavior and repeated infection with veneral disease] *Srpski arhiv za celokupno lekarstvo, 127* (7-8), 254-257.

Bluebook, (2014). Retrieved from: http:// www.who.int/ classifications/ icd/ en/bluebook.pdf.

CAmom, (2015). Libido in recovering alcoholic males? Retrieved from: https:// answers.yahoo.com/ question/ index?qid=20130417185615 AAXd 97Q.

Cooper, L. (2010). Does Drinking Promote Risky Sexual Behavior?: A Complex Answer to a Simple Question. In T. D. Fisher, & J. McNulty (Eds.). *Current directions in human sexuality and intimate relationships*, (pp. 19-23). Boston: Allyn & Bacon.

Cooper, M. L. (2002). Alcohol use and risky sexual behavior among college students and youth. *Journal of Studies on Alcohol, 14*(Suppl.), 101–117.

Cottencin, O. (2009). [Severe depression and addictions] (in French). *Encephale, 35*, Suppl 7, 264–268.

Dependence syndrome. Retrieved from: http:// www.who.int/ substance_ abuse/terminology/definition1/en/.

DSM-V, (2013). *Diagnostic and Statistical Manual of Mental Disorders, 5th Edition*. Washington, DC: APA.

Eysenck, H. J. (1976). *Sex and personality*. London: Open Books.

Falk, D. E., Yi, H. Y. & Hilton, M. E. (2008). Age of onset and temporal sequencing of lifetime DSM-IV alcohol use disorders relative to comorbid mood and anxiety disorders. *Drug and Alcohol Dependence, 94* (1–3), 234–245.

Farris, C., Treat, T. A. & Viken, R. J. (2010). Alcohol alters men's perceptual and decisional processing of women's sexual interest. *Journal of Abnormal Psychology, 119*(2), 427-432.

Gelder, M. G., López-Ibor, J. J. jr, & Andreasen, N. C. (2004). *New Oxford textbook of psychiatry*. Oxford: Oxford University Press.

Gilmore, A. K., George, W. H., Nguyen, H. V., Heiman, J. R., Davis, K. C. & Norris, J. (2013). Influences of situational factors and alcohol expectancies on sexual desire and arousal among heavy-episodic drinking women: acute alcohol intoxication and condom availability. *Archives of Sexual Behavior*, *42*(6), 949-959.

Gpnotebook, (2014). Retrieved from http:// www.gpnotebook.co.uk/ simplepage.cfm?ID=x20091123152205182440.

Graziottin, A. (1998). The biological basis of female sexuality. *International Clinical Psychopharmacology*, *13*, Suppl 6, 15-22.

Heiser, K. & Hartmann, U. (1987). Disorders of sexual desire in a sample of women alcoholics. *Drug and Alcohol Dependence*, *19*(2), 145-157.

Janicak, P. G., Marder, S. R. & Pavuluri, M. N. (2011). *Principles and practice of psychopharmacotherap*. Philadelphia: Wolters Kluwer Health/ Lippincott Williams Wilkins., pp. 507–508.

Jensen, S. B. (1984). Sexual Function and dysfunction in younger married alcoholics: a comparative study. *Acta Psychiatrica Scandinavica*, *69*(6), 543-549.

Kaplan, H. I. & Sadock, B. J. (Eds.) (1989). *Comprehensive Textbook of Psychiatry / V.* Vol. *1*, *fifth edition*. Baltimore - Hong Kong - London - Sydney: Williams&Wilkins.

Kiefer, D. (2012). Depression and sexual health. Retireved from: http:// www. healthline.com/health/depression/sexual-health.

Kobayashi, T., Hayakawa, S., Matsuda, M., Tsuchida, H., Haga, H., Tani, N. & Fukui, K. (1999). [Mental and physical symptoms in alcoholics after alcohol withdrawal--comparing with involutional melancholia patients]. *Nihon Arukoru Yakubutsu Igakkai Zasshi*, *34*(6), 558-567.

Lamovec, T. (1980). [*Psychology of motivation, emotions, personality amd learning – an experimental manual*] (in slovene). Ljubljana: Filozofska fakulteta.

Leigh, B. C. & Stall, R. (1993). Substance use and risky sexual behavior for exposure to HIV: Issues in methodology. *American Psychologist*, *48*, 1035–1045.

Lin, D., Li, X., Yang, H., Fang, X., Stanton, B., Chen, X., Abbey, A. & Lui, H. (2005). Alcohol intoxication and sexual risk behaviors among rural-tourban. *Drug and Alcohol Dependence*, *79*, 103-112.

Logue, P. E., Gentry W. D., Linnoila, M. & Erwin C. W. (1978). Effect of Alcohol Consumption on State Anxiety Changes in Male and Female Nonalcoholics. *American Journal of Psychiatry*, *135*, 1079–1081.

Loper, R. G., Kammeier M. L. & Hoffmann, H. (1973). M.M.P.I. Characteristics of College Freshman Males Who Later Became Alcoholics. *Journal of Abnormal Psychology*, *82*, 159–162.

Mack, A. H., Harrington, A. L. & Frances, R. J. (2010). *Clinical manual for treatment of alcoholism and addictions.* Washington: American Psychiatric Publishing.

Martin, R. L., Cloninger, C. R. & Guze, S. B. (1984). The longitudinal course of alcoholism among women criminals: a six-year follow-up. In D. W. Goodwin, K. T. Van Dusen, & S. A. Mednick (Eds.), *Alcoholism – Longitudinal studies*, (pp. 39-52). Boston: Kluwer-Nijhoff.

Mashman, R. C. (1997). An evolutionary view of psychic misery. *Journal of Social Behaviour & Personality*, *12*, 979–999.

McNamee, H. B., Mendelson, J. H. & Mello, N. K. (1968). Experimental Analysis of Drinking Patterns of Alcoholics: Concurrent Psychiatric Observations. *American Journal of Psychiatry*, *124*, 1063–1069.

Mike, O. (2008). Decreased libido. Retrieved from: http://www.e-aa.org/forum/viewtopic.php?f=21&t=4490.

Miller, N. S. & Gold, M. S. (1988). The human sexual response and alcohol and drugs. *Journal of Substance Abuse Treatment*, *5*(3), 171-177.

Nathan, P. E., Titler N. A., Lowenstein L. M., Solomon P. & Rossi A. M. (1970). Behavioral Analysis of Chronic Alcoholism. *Archives of General Psychiatry*, *22*, 419–430.

Purdie, M. P., Norris, J., Davis, K. C., Zawacki, T., Morrison, D. M., George, W. H. & Kiekel, P. A. (2011). The effects of acute alcohol intoxication, partner risk level, and general intention to have unprotected sex on women's sexual decision making with a new partner. *Experimental and Clinical Psychopharmacology*, *19*, 378-88.

Roman, P. M. (1988). Biological features of woman's alcohol use: a review. *Public Health Reports*, *103*(6), 628-637.

Rubenstein, C. (1989). The Baby bomb. New York *Times Magazine*, *October 8*. Retrieved from: http:// www.nytimes.com/ 1989/ 10/ 08/ magazine/ the-baby-bomb.html.

Shakespeare, W. (1606/2014). Retrieved from: http:// www.bartleby.com/ 46/ 4/ 23.html.

Seki, M., Yoshida, K. & Okamura, Y. (1991). [A study on hyperprolactinemia in female pacients with alcoholics]. *Arukoru Kenkyuto Yakubutsu Ison*, *26*(1), 49-59.

Selzer, M. L. (1980). Alcoholism and Alcoholic Psychoses. In H. I. Kaplan, A. M. Freedman, & B. J. Sadock (Eds.), *Comprehensive Textbook of Psychiatry III*, Vol. *2* (pp. 1629-1645). Baltimore: Williams and Wilkins.

Strauss Turner, D. & Dudek, F. A. (1982). An analysis of alcoholism and its effects on sexual functioning. *Sexuality and Disability*, *5*(3), 143-157.

Tamerin, J. S., Weiner, S. & Mendelson, J. H. (1970). Alcoholics' Expectancies and Recall of Experiences During Intoxication. *American Journal of Psychiatry*, *26*(12), 1697-1704.

The Cleveland Clinic Foundation, (2015). Sexual problems and depression. Retireved from: http://my.clevelandclinic.org/ services/ neurological_ institute/center-for-behavorial-health/disease-conditions/hic-sexual-problems-depression.

The ICD-10 Classification of Mental and Behavioural Disorders: Clinical descriptions and diagnostic guidelines: Retrieved from: http:// www. who.int/substance_abuse/terminology/ICD10ClinicalDiagnosis.pdf.

Tzambazis, K. & Stough, C. (2000). Alcohol impairs speed of information processing and simple and choice reaction time and differentially impairs higher-order cognitive abilities, *Alochol & Alcoholism*, *35*, 197-201.

Vaillant, G. E. (1995). *The natural history of alcoholism revisited.* Cambridge, MA: Harvard University Press.

Vijayasenan, M. E. (1981). Alcohol and sex. *The New Zealand Medical Journal*, *93*(675), 18-20.

Webber, C. (2015). Depression – how it affects sex and relationships. Retrieved from: http:// www.netdoctor.co.uk/ sex_relationships/ facts/ depressrelation.htm.

Židanik, M. & Čebašek-Travnik, Z. (2003). [*The syndrome of alcohol dependence*] (in slovene). Maribor: Dispanzer za zdravljenje alkoholizma in drugih odvisnosti, Zdravstveni dom dr. Adolfa Drolca; Ljubljana: Psihiatrična klinika.

Biographical Sketch

Aleš Friedl

He was born in 1961 in Ptuj, Slovenia.

He studied psychology at the University of Ljubljana from which he graduated in 1985. In 1991 he obtained his M.Sc. degree. In the year 2006 he obtained his Ph.D. degree in the field of psychology.

He started working as a psychologist for the purpose of personnel selection at a construction company. There he also practised psycho diagnostics and research.

In 1991 he started working in the Psychiatric hospital Ormož. In 1996 he completed his specialisation (course) in clinical psychology. Since then he has been treating addicts.

In 1998 Vili Trofenk, the mayor of the municipality of Ormož appointed him a member of the Local action group for preventing addiction for the period of five years. He presented the results of this programme at various round tables and gave some lectures for students and parents at different schools. He was again appointed several times. He worked as a member of this group till 2011.

Since 2006 he has been working as a forensic psychologist. In 2015 he assessed the first accused Slovenian healthcare serial killer.

Since 2008 he has been an assistant in Department of Psychology at Faculty of Arts, University of Maribor. Since 2011 he has been a higher education lecturer at Alma Mater Europaea – European Centre Maribor.

Selected Bibliography

1. FRIEDL, Aleš. Abuse of psychoactive substances at work in the aspect of legal regulation (in slovene). *Podjetje in delo*, 2000, Vol. 26, No. 8, pp. 1665-1671.
2. FRIEDL, Aleš. Personality disorders in the light of Kernberger's theory (in slovene). *Revija za kriminalistiko in kriminologijo*, 2006, Vol. 57, No. 4, pp. 349-358.
3. FRIEDL, Aleš. Aristotle's opinions of addiction. *Alcoholism (Zagreb)*, 2007, Vol. 43, No. 2, pp. 119-125.
4. FRIEDL, Aleš. Intermunicipal local action group (LAS) for preventing addictions in the districts of communities Ormož. *Alcoholism (Zagreb)*, 2008, Vol. 44, Suppl. 1, pp. 80-81.
5. FRIEDL, Aleš. What do jokes on alcoholics tell us about alcoholism. *Alcoholism (Zagreb)*, 2012, Vol. 48, No. 1, pp. 23-40.
6. FRIEDL, Aleš. Is the autcome of alcohol dependence treatment related to intelligence of patients? *Alcoholism (Zagreb)*, 2014, Vol. 50, No. 1, pp. 13-23.
7. FRIEDL, Aleš. Preparing oneself to pass the anatomy exam: a case report. In: PLENKOVIĆ, Mario (ur.), GALIČIĆ, Vlado (ur.), TOPLAK, Ludvik (ur.). *Society and technology 2014 - dr. Juraj Plenković: book of manuscripts*. Zagreb: Croatian Communication Association, 2014, pp. 290-291.

In: Substance Abuse
Editor: Tanya Reid
ISBN: 978-1-63485-612-6

Chapter 4

ASSESSING MIRTAZAPINE AS A POSSIBLE TREATMENT OPTION IN COMORBID MAJOR DEPRESSION/ALCOHOL USE DISORDER: TWO PILOT STUDIES

Jack R. Cornelius**, MD, MPH, Ihsan M. Salloum, MD, MPH, Antoine Douaihy, MD, Tammy Chung, PhD, Jody Glance, MD, Julie Kmiec, DO, Maribeth A. Wesesky, CMA, Douglas Fitzgerald, BA, and Levent Kirisci, PhD

University of Pittsburgh, Pittsburgh, PA, US

ABSTRACT

This report summarizes the results of our two double-blind, placebo-controlled pilot studies conducted in order to evaluate the efficacy of mirtazapine for the treatment of persons with comorbid major depressive disorder and an alcohol use disorder (MDD/AUD). The first of these studies has been completed, but the second study, which involved a younger treatment sample, remains ongoing, so outcome data concerning the second study is mostly limited to a presentation of side effects that have been noted to date in that study. To our knowledge, these were the

* Corresponding author: Jack R. Cornelius. E-mail: corneliusjr@upmc.edu.

first two studies to evaluate the efficacy of the novel antidepressant mirtazapine for treating both the depressive symptoms and the level of alcohol consumption of persons with comorbid major depression and an alcohol use disorder (MDD/AUD), since previous studies involving mirtazapine in MDD/AUD did not assess the level of alcohol consumption. Mirtazapine was well tolerated in both of our studies, with few side effects and with no serious adverse events. The results of the first study showed a significant within-group decrease in depressive symptoms by week 2, which was also noted at all subsequent assessments (weeks 3, 4, 6, 8, 10, and 12) during the 12-week study. However, no evidence of efficacy was sound for mirtazapine for decreasing the level of alcohol consumption of MDD/AUD subjects. Also, no significant between-group differences in level of either depressive symptoms or of alcohol consumption was noted in either study, perhaps because of limited sample size. Further studies are warranted to assess the efficacy of mirtazapine for treating comorbid populations.

1. Introduction

Mirtazapine is a second generation antidepressant with a tetracyclic structure. It is unique in its structure and in its pharmacological profile, and is unrelated to tricyclic antidepressants or SSRI antidepressants. Mirtazapine has been thought to be a potentially promising medication for treating comorbid populations because mirtazapine has been reported to be superior to other antidepressant medications for treating depression in a large meta-analysis of non-comorbid depressed subjects in studies involving new-generation antidepressants (Cipriani et al., 2009).

Results from two previous existing studies conducted outside of the United States (in South Korea and in Turkey, respectively) suggest efficacy for the structurally and functionally unique antidepressant mirtazapine for decreasing the depressive symptoms of persons with comorbid major depressive disorder (MDD) and an alcohol use disorder (AUD) (Yoon et al., 2006; Altintoprak et al., 2008). However, the Yoon et al., 2006 study did not utilize a placebo control group, and neither of those two studies assessed level of alcohol consumption during the studies, so efficacy of mirtazapine for decreasing level of alcohol consumption could not be assessed. Therefore, the therapeutic potential of mirtazapine among comorbid populations remains unclear.

2. Method

2.1. Subjects

Recently, we conducted two pilot studies funded by the NIH designed to assess the efficacy of mirtazapine for decreasing the depressive symptoms and the level of alcohol use of adults and of late adolescents/young adults. The first of these studies has been completed, but the second study, which involved a younger treatment sample, remains ongoing. We hypothesized that mirtazapine would be safe in those populations and would be associated with decreases in depressive symptoms and alcohol consumption. Both of these two recent studies involved 12-week double-blind, placebo-controlled trials. The first study involved 14 adults between the ages of 18 and 55, while the second study involved 6 persons (so far) between the ages of 18 and 30. The two studies utilized very similar methodology except for the age range of the participants. The diagnoses of MDD and AUD were made using the MINI International Neuropsychiatric Interview (Sheehan et al., 1998). Inclusion criteria included a diagnosis of MDD and a diagnosis of AUD. Both current MDD and current AUD had to be present in order to meet inclusion criteria for the study. Exclusion criteria included: age less than 18 years of age or over 55 years of age; use of psychotropic medication in the prior month; presence of a diagnosis involving psychosis or psychotic symptoms; DSM diagnosis of dependence or abuse on substances other than alcohol, cannabis, caffeine, or nicotine; positive pregnancy test or breastfeeding; significant neurological or medical condition; or inability to read or understand study forms.

2.2. Pharmacotherapy

Written informed consent was obtained from all potential subjects after all study procedures had been fully explained before entry into the study. Both studies were approved by the University of Pittsburgh Institutional Review Board (IRB). Both studies involved a double-blind, placebo-controlled study design. The medication trial lasted 12 weeks. The protocol medication was taken once each day at bedtime. The mirtazapine and placebo were given by the research pharmacy in identically-appearing capsules. Subjects were given a starting dose of 15 mg of mirtazapine or one tablet of placebo for the first two weeks of trial, and then the dose was increased to 30 mg of mirtazapine or two tablets of placebo for the remainder of the trial.

2.3. Motivational Enhancement Therapy

Motivational Enhancement Therapy was also provided to all subjects in both studies (Miller et al., 1992). MET is a brief intervention used to enhance an individual's engagement in therapy and motivation to make changes regarding alcohol use and related problems, such as depression. Therapy was provided by trained staff who had years of experience in providing protocol therapy to subjects of NIH research studies.

2.4. Assessment Procedures and Measures

Level of alcohol consumption was evaluated using the timeline follow-back method (TLFB) (Sobell et al. 1988). Level of participant-rated depressive symptoms was assessed using the Beck Depression Inventory (BDI) (Beck et al., 1961). Level of alcohol craving was assessed using the Obsessive Compulsive Drinking Scale (Anton, 2000). Level of medication side effects was assessed using the Systematic Assessment for Treatment Emergent Events-systematic Inquire (SAFTEE/SI) (Levine et al. 1986). All ratings were performed by staff members who had been specially trained with the study instruments and who had years of experience in conducting assessments with comorbid subjects in NIH studies.

2.5. Statistical Analysis

Descriptive statistics were first calculated for all variables. Paired t tests and analysis of variance were utilized to compare continuous baseline measures. Categorical baseline measures were compared using chi-square analysis, corrected for continuity. Outcome measures were assessed using repeated measures ANOVA and by paired t tests. Race and gender were assess as covariates. Statistical analyses were performed using an intent-to-treat study design. All test of significance were 2-tailed. Statistical significance was indicated by an alpha level of ≤ 0.05. Analyses were performed using the Statistical Package for the Social Sciences, version 23.0 (IBM Corp, 2014).

3. RESULTS

A total of 14 persons participated in the study, including 7 who had been randomized to mirtazapine and 7 who had been randomized to placebo. Ten other potential subjects had been ruled out at the baseline evaluation. Study subjects included ten (71%) men and 4 (29%) women. There were no significant differences between the mirtazapine group and the placebo group in distribution of any demographic variables or variables used as outcome measures. At baseline, subjects demonstrated prominent alcohol consumption, drinking five or more drinks per day on 48% of days, and all also demonstrated moderate to severe levels of depressive symptoms on the Beck Depression Inventory.

Mirtazapine was well tolerated in these studies, with increased weight being the only medication side effect which occurred more frequently in the mirtazapine group than in the placebo group. The mirtazapine group gained an average of 5.2 pounds during the course of the study compared to a gain of 1.3 pounds in the placebo group. No serious adverse events were noted in either medication trial. All subjects in both treatment groups of both studies showed clinical improvements in both depressive symptoms and in level of drinking during their study participation. In the adult study, within-group t tests in the mirtazapine group showed a significant decrease in BDI depressive symptoms by week 2, which were also noted at all subsequent assessments (weeks 3, 4, 6, 8, 10, and 12). In contrast, no significant within-group decrease in depressive symptoms was noted in the placebo group until week 8. In the adult study, both treatment groups showed statistically significant decreases in both depressive symptoms and in level of alcohol consumption by the end of the study, but no significant between-group differences were noted in either depressive symptoms or in level of alcohol consumption, though a trend toward greater improvement in depression was noted in the mirtazapine group of the adult study at week 4. Alcohol craving showed a significant decrease during the course of the study in both treatment groups, but no significant between-group difference was noted. The second study, which is the study involving the younger study population of adolescents and young adults remains ongoing, so information from that study is limited.

Some secondary analyses were also conducted involving symptoms related to drinking and depression. It was noted that improvements in depressive symptoms were prominent in both treatment groups in this study, while improvements in drinking were somewhat smaller. It was noted that changes in depressive symptoms tended to precede the changes in drinking, especially in the mirtazapine group. It was noted that changes in depressive symptoms were significantly associated with drinking intensity (drinks per drinking day), but were not associated with changes in frequency of drinking. Suicidal ideation was rare in the study, and was slightly lower in the mirtazapine group than in the placebo group, though the difference was not statistically significant. No subject made a suicide attempt during the course of the study, and none demonstrated prominent suicidal ideations during the course of the study. The most common sleep problem at the start of the study was sleep continuity disturbance rather than difficulty falling asleep or early morning awakening, which is a common pattern among person with an AUD. Sleep problems improved in both treatment groups during the course of the study, with most of the improvement occurring during the first few weeks of the study. Three persons used low level of cannabis at the start of the study, and all three of those persons happened to be in the mirtazapine group. Two of those persons had completely stopped using cannabis by the second half of the study. Nine of the 14 subjects who participated in the study were employed full time or part-time at baseline, and five were not employed. During the course of the study, three of those five persons who had been unemployed became employed during the course of the study, and no participant lost their jobs during the course of the study.

During the course of the study, some additional observations were made regarding the methodology of the two studies, as compared to the methodology of the studies that we conducted in the past. For example, electronic recruitment methods were noted to help increase recruitment in the studies currently being described, using techniques such as using web sites. That technique was particularly helpful for recruiting younger participants. Electronic reminders for appointments were also used by our research group for the first time during this study, using methods such as text messaging, and those methods were found to be helpful, especially for younger participants. On the other hand, traditional hard copy forms of recruitment, such as campus newspapers, and traditional reminders of appointments appeared to be less effective than in our past studies conducted ten or twenty years ago, especially for younger participants (Cornelius et al., 1997; Cornelius et al., 2009).

Conclusion

The preliminary observations noted in this study suggest that mirtazapine is safe in persons with comorbid MDD/AUD. Within-group findings from this study suggest possible efficacy for mirtazapine for decreasing the depressive symptoms of persons with comorbid MDD/AUD. However, no between-group efficacy was noted for mirtazapine for treating either the depressive symptoms or the alcohol consumption of MDD/AUD individuals. The lack of a significant between-group difference may reflect the limited sample size of the current study, which was only powered to detect large effect size changes. It is noteworthy that subjects in the placebo group demonstrated significant improvements in depressive symptoms and in levels of alcohol consumption during the course of the study, just as was noted in the mirtazapine group. The clinical improvement noted in both depressive symptoms and in level of alcohol consumption in the placebo group may have resulted from the MET therapy that they received during the course of the study, which appeared to be a broad and powerful therapeutic factor in our previous pharmacotherapy studies involving comorbid populations (Cornelius et al., 2011).

The results of the two recent mirtazapine trials that are currently being presented can be compared with the results of our previous large double-blind, placebo-controlled NIH treatment trials involving the SSRI antidepressant fluoxetine in participants with MDD/AUD (Cornelius et al., 2009). That study demonstrated no efficacy for fluoxetine for treating either the alcohol consumption or the depressive symptoms of outpatients with co-occurring MDD/AUD. On the other hand, our current study involving mirtazapine suggests possible efficacy for mirtazapine for decreasing the depressive symptoms of that comorbid population, though no clear efficacy for treating alcohol consumption was shown in either study.

Further larger studies are warranted to more definitively evaluate the efficacy of mirtazapine for treating comorbid MDD/AUD, and to evaluate the influences of demographic and clinical factors in predicting treatment outcome. Further studies are also warranted to assess the efficacy of mirtazapine among inpatient populations with comorbid MDD/AUD.

Sources of funding: Supported by R21 AA022123, R21 AA022863, K24 AA015320, R01 DA019142, and P50 DA05605.

References

Altintoprak, A.E., Zorlu, N., Coskunol, H., Akdeniz, F., Kitapcioglu, G. (2008). Effectiveness and tolerability of mirtazapine and amitriptyline in alcoholic patients with co-morbid depressive disorder: A randomized, double-blind study. *Human Psychopharmacology*, 23, 313-319.

Ambrosini, P.J., Metz, C., Bianchi, M.D., Rabinovich, H., Undie, A. (1991). Concurrent validity and psychometric properties of the Beck Depression Inventory in outpatient adolescents. *Journal of the American Academy of Child and Adolescent. Psychiatry*, 30, 51-57.

Anton, R.F. (2000). Obsessive-compulsive aspects of craving: Development of the Obsessive Compulsive Drinking Scale. *Addiction*, 95, Supl. 2, S211-S 117.

Beck, A.T., Ward, C.H., Mendelson, M., Mock, J., and Erbaugh, J. (1961). An inventory for measuring depression. *Archives of General Psychiatry*, 4, 561-571.

Cipriani, A., Furukawa, T.A., Salanti, G., Geddes, J.R., Higgins, J.P., Churchill, R., Barbui, C. (2009). Comparative efficacy and acceptability of 12 new-generation antidepressants: A multiple-treatments meta-analysis. *Lancet*, 373, 746-758.

Cornelius, J.R., Bukstein, O.G., Douaihy, A.B., Clark, D.B., Chung, T.A., Daley, D.C., Wood, D.S., Brown, S.J. (2010). Double-blind fluoxetine trial in comorbid MDD-CUD youth and young adults. *Drug and Alcohol Dependence*, 112, 39-45.

Cornelius, J.R., Bukstein, O., Salloum, I., and Clark, D. (2005). Treatment of co-occurring alcohol, drug, and psychiatric disorders, Chapter 16, in volume XVII entitled Alcohol Problems in Adolescents and Young Adults, in the series of books entitled Recent Developments in Alcoholism, Marc Galanter (ed.), Kluwer Academic/Plenum Publishers, New York, 349-366.

Cornelius, J.R., Bukstein, O.G., Wood, D.S., Kirisci, L. Douaihy, A.B., Clark, D.B. (2009). Double-blind placebo-controlled trial of fluoxetine in adolescents with comorbid major depression and an alcohol use disorder. *Addictive Behaviors*, 34, 905-909.

Cornelius, J.R., and Clark, D.B. (2007). Translational research involving adolescent substance abuse, Chapter 16, in the book entitled *Translation of Addiction Science into Practice: Update and Future Directions*, Peter Miller and David Kavanagh (eds.), Elsevier Press, New York, NY, 341-360.

Cornelius, J.R., Douaihy, A.B., Bukstein, O.D., Daley, D.C., Wood, D.S., Kelly, T.M., Salloum, I.M. (2011). Evaluation of cognitive behavioral therapy/motivation enhancement therapy (CBT/MET) in a treatment trial of comorbid alcohol use disorder/major depressive disorder adolescents. *Addictive Behaviors*, 36, 843-848.

Cornelius, J.R., Douaihy, A.B., Clark, D.B., Chung, T, Wood D.S., Daley, D. (2012). Mirtazapine in comorbid major depression and alcohol dependence: An open-label trial. *Journal of Dual Diagnosis*, 8, 2000-2004.

Cornelius, J.R., Salloum, I.M., Ehler, J.G., Jarrett, P.J., Cornelius, M.D., Perel, J.M., Thase, M.E., Black, A. (1997). Fluoxetine in depressed alcoholics: A double-blind, placebo-controlled trial. *Archives of General Psychiatry*, 54, 700-705.

IBM Corp. Released (2014). *IBM SPSS Statistics for Windows*, Version 23.0. IBM Corp. Armonk, NY.

Levine, J., Schooler, R.N. (1986). SAFTEE: A technique for the systematic assessment of side effects in clinical trials. *Psychopharmacology Bulletin*, 22, 343-381.

Lovieno, N., Tedeschini, E., Bentley, K.H., Evins, A.E., Papakostas, G.I. (2011). Antidepressants for major depressive disorder and dysthymic disorder in patients with comorbid alcohol use disorders: A meta-analysis of placebo-controlled randomized trials. *Journal of Clinical Psychiatry*, 72, 1144-1151.

MacKenzie, I.S. (2013). Within-subjects vs. between-subjects designs: Which to use? Chapter 5, In: *Human-Computer Interaction: An Empirical Research Perspective*. Waltham, MA: Morgan Kaufmann.

Miller, W.R., Zweben, A., DiClemente, C.C., Rychtarik, R.G. (1992). *Motivational Enhancement Therapy Manual. Project MATCH Monograph Series*, Volume 2. Washington, DC: National Institute on Alcohol Abuse and Alcoholism.

Nunes, E.V., Levin, F.B. (2004). Treatment of depression in patients with alcohol or other drug dependence. A meta-analysis. *Journal of the American Medical Association (JAMA)*, 291, 1887-1896.

Sheehan, D.V., Lecrubier, Y., Sheehan, H., Amorim, P., Janars, J., Weiller, E., Dunbar, G.C. (1998). The Mini-International Neuropsychiatric Interview (MINI): The development and validation of a structured diagnostic psychiatric interview for DSM-IV and ICD-10. *Journal of Clinical Psychiatry*, 59, supl. 20, 22-33.

Sobell, L.D., Sobell, M.B., Leo, G.I., and Cancilla, A. (1988). Reliability of a timeline method: Assessing normal drinkers' reports of recent drinking and a comparative evaluation across several populations. *British Journal of Addiction*, 83, 393-402.

Watanabe, N., Omori, I.M., Nakagawa, A., Cipriani, A., Barbui, C., McGuire, H., Furukawa, T.A. (2008). Mirtazapine versus other antidepressants in the acute-phase treatment of adults with major depression: Systematic review and meta-analysis. *Journal of Clinical Psychiatry*, 69, 1404-1415.

Yoon, S.J., Pae, C.U., Kim, D.J., Namkoong, K., Lee, E., Oh, D.Y., Lee, C.T. (2006). Mirtazapine for patients with alcohol dependence and comorbid depressive disorders: A multicentre, open label study. *Progress in Neuro-Psychopharmacology and Biological Psychiatry*, 30, 1196-1201.

In: Substance Abuse
Editor: Tanya Reid
ISBN: 978-1-63485-612-6

Chapter 5

BEATING THE SCENE: A RE-OFFENSE PREVENTION PROGRAM FOR DELINQUENTS SUFFERING FROM SUBSTANCE USE DISORDERS

Ron van Outsem*[*], *PhD
Inforsa-Arkin, Amsterdam, The Netherlands

ABSTRACT

In this chapter, a re-offense prevention program is presented which specifically addresses the participant's social network composition. Beating the Scene, as the program is called, is a protocolized program that makes ample use of cognitive behavioral therapeutic techniques. This program has five main goals: 1: The creation of awareness of the negative influences of the participant's criminogenic peer group, 2: The enhancement of the participant's motivation to build up a prosocial network, 3: The design of a personalized and rewarding prosocial network, 4: The acquisition of the necessary social skills, and 5: The buddy-assisted introduction of participants into existing prosocial networks.

Beating the Scene can be used in both inpatient and outpatient settings. It can be added to a wide array of forensic treatment regimens for patients suffering from SUDs.

[*] Ron van Outsem email: ronvanoutsem@casema.nl.

Keywords: substance use disorders, buddy-assisted program, prosocial network, re-offence prevention

Introduction

Substance Use Disorders (SUDs) are known to be important contributing factors to the development and exacerbation of various types of antisocial and delinquent behavior. The treatment of patients who exhibit frequent antisocial behavior and suffer from these conditions is often experienced as challenging by therapists and usually produce very modest effects, if any at all.

One of the most important statistical predictors of criminal recidivism and of relapse to substance use in delinquents suffering from SUDs is having a social network predominantly consisting of people who also use alcohol and/or drugs, and who also engage in criminal activities (Beattie & Longabaugh, 1999; Berg & Huebner, 2011; Brewer et al., 1998; Dobkin et al., 2002; Ennet et al., 2006; Hipp et al., 2010; Marlatt & Witkiewitz, 2005; McIntosh & McKeganey, 2000; Pearson & Michell, 2000). Another important predictor is the experience of loneliness resulting from the absence of an adequate social support network (Levy, 2008; Rachlin, 2000; Skog, 2003; Tate et al., 2004). In order to reduce relapse and criminal recidivism rates in these patients, it is paramount to address their social network architecture. Interventions should be aimed at enabling these patients to abandon their criminogenic peer group and to build up a rewarding prosocial network.

In this chapter, a re-offense prevention program is presented which specifically addresses the patient's social network composition. Beating the Scene, as the program is called, is a protocolized program that makes ample use of cognitive behavioral therapeutic techniques. It aims at the development of a prosocial network by the participant through the achievement of the following five goals: 1: The creation of awareness of the negative influences of the participant's criminogenic peer group, 2: The enhancement of the participant's motivation to build up a prosocial network, 3: The design of a personalized and rewarding prosocial network, 4: The acquisition of the necessary social skills, and 5: The buddy-assisted introduction of participants into existing prosocial networks. The achievement of the first four goals can regarded as a preparation phase of the building of a prosocial network. In order to achieve the fifth and final goal, what is learned in the preparation phase is put into practice and the participant's prosocial network is actually built.

Beating the Scene can be used in both inpatient and outpatient settings. It can be added to a wide array of forensic treatment regimens for patients suffering from SUDs. Total abstinence is not a critical requirement for participation, but (at least some) motivation for positive change is.

PHASE 1, THE PREPARATION PHASE

The first phase of the Beating the Scene program consists of a series of individual or group sessions in which nine steps are to be taken. These steps are:

1. The introduction of the participants into the program.
2. The creation of awareness of the influences of the participant's criminogenic peer group.
3. The enhancement of the ability to recognize prosocial people and to designate finding places of prosocial people.
4. The enhancement of motivation in the participant to develop a prosocial network by creating awareness of the advantages of being part of such a social network.
5. The design of a prosocial network that matches the participant's personality, needs, and preferences.
6. The exploration of the participant's own possibilities and skills to develop a rewarding prosocial network.
7. The acquisition of relevant social skills.
8. The preparation of the participant for the buddy-assisted part of the program.
9. Making a Prosocial Network Plan.

The sessions should be held at least once a week in order to reduce attrition.

The number of sessions needed to complete this phase of the program is not necessarily fixed. Rather, it deserves preference to thoroughly complete each step before moving on to the next one.

Group sessions should take place with a fixed group of participants in order for them to be able to work through all of the program's steps together and simultaneously.

All participants receive a workbook which contains relevant information for each step of the program and assignments to complete either within the session or at home. This workbook serves as a guide that leads the participant through the first phase of the program. In the next paragraphs of this chapter, directions are given as to how to compose such a workbook. It is chosen not to present a fixed or compulsory format for this workbook in order to give therapists the freedom to adjust the workbook to the specific characteristics and needs of the group of patients that is treated.

The Prosocial Network Workbook

The Prosocial Network Workbook should contain relevant information for the participants to read and discuss in preparation for or during the sessions. This information is easily found on the internet and in the available literature on the subject of interpersonal relations and social interaction. It is important to rewrite this information in such a form that it becomes easily readable and comprehensible for the patients who participate in the program. Cultural aspects should also be taken into account when writing the text of the workbook since accepted and unacceptable forms of social interaction vary from culture to culture.

The workbook is composed of nine chapters, each corresponding to each of the nine steps of the first phase of the program. Every chapter, or step, is divided in three parts:

A. A synopsis of the theme that will be discussed and worked with.
B. One or more assignments to complete during the session.
C. Homework assignments that will be discussed at the beginning of the next session.

Extra relevant information can be offered in appendices at the end of the workbook.

Finally, it is always advisable to give the workbook an attractive cover and to print it in color and on good quality paper. Professional-looking material is often taken more seriously and is usually less often lost or forgotten.

STEP 1: INTRODUCTION

A: Synopsis

In the first session of the program, the participant is introduced to the therapists, to his or her fellow participants, and to the program itself. The way this is done depends on the culture and customs of the participants and on the preferences of the therapists. The important thing is to create a positive group environment in which mutual acceptance, support, and collaboration is possible.

When introducing the participants to the program, the following elements are important:

1. Highlighting the main goal of the program.
2. Informing the participants about how the program works and about what is expected of the participants.

1: Highlighting the Main Goal of the Program

First of all, it should be explained to the participants that having friends or acquaintances who are involved in substance use and/or in criminal activities is a strong predictor of their own relapse in substance use and of their own criminal recidivism. In order to reduce the risk of relapse and re-offending, it is therefore paramount to reform one's social network. The achievement of this reform is the main goal of the program. While explaining this, it is useful to give concrete examples of how people can be influenced by others and of how they can be persuaded to do things they don't really want to do and often regret afterwards.

Secondly, it is important for the participants to get a clear understanding of what prosocial and antisocial people are. Therefore, both types of people should be defined as to their main characteristics. A helpful tool for creating a consensus among the participants on these definitions is letting them add, delete or change statements in Table 1.

2: Informing the Participants about How the Program Works and about What Is Expected of the Participants

In this part of the session, the complete program is explained step by step. The techniques that are used are also discussed. It is important to stress that the first phase of the program serves as a theoretical preparation for the second phase, in which the actual building of a prosocial network will take place.

An active participation during the sessions is expected from all participants. They must also be informed about the basic rules of participation, preferably in writing. These rules relate to attendance, punctuality, safety, mutual respect, sobriety during sessions, and confidentiality.

B: Assignment

Reflection on the Program by the Participants by Discussing Their Goals, Thoughts, Feelings and Hesitations about Building up a Prosocial Network

The last part of the first session is spent by the participants discussing the information they have received and their personal motivations and hesitations about reforming their social network. The purpose of this discussion is to enhance the motivation of the participants.

Table 1.

Prosocial people (people who are good for me)...	Antisocial people (people who are bad for me, "toxic" friendships)...
Don't do drugs*	Do drugs
Don't *abuse* alcohol*	Abuse alcohol
Don't do crime*	Do crime
Help others	Think only about themselves
Make something of their lives	Waste their lives
Are an asset to their community	Parasitize on their community
Respect others and their opinions	Don't care about others/like to hurt others
Are interested in sharing with others	Are interested in taking from others
Are trustworthy	Can't be trusted
....	....
....	....
....	....
....	....

* These statements cannot be changed or deleted.

The therapists are encouraged to make use of motivational interviewing techniques as described by Miller and Rollnick (2002). This is not only the case in the course of this assignment, but also throughout the whole program.

At the end of the discussion, the participants are asked to write down their main conclusions in their workbooks.

C: Homework

For homework, the participants are asked to reflect on the conclusions of the previous session and to write down in their workbooks their personal motives for completing the program and for reforming their social networks.

Step 2: The Creation of Awareness of the Influences of the Participant's Criminogenic Peer Group

A: Synopsis

In this step of the program, the participants are made aware of the influences of their present social network on their thoughts, opinions, attitudes, emotions, substance use, and (general and criminal) behavior. An important tool for the creation of this awareness is the sociogram. A sociogram is a graphic representation of social links that a person has. It is a graph drawing that plots the structure of interpersonal relations in a group situation. Sociograms were developed by Jacob L. Moreno (1934) to analyze choices or preferences within a group. They can diagram the structure and patterns of group interactions. A sociogram can be drawn on the basis of many different criteria: Social relations, channels of influence, lines of communication, etc. There are many types of sociograms (Russel & Cohn, 2015). It is up to the therapists to choose which type of sociogram is used. Whatever type of sociogram is chosen, the sociogram should at least depict:

- Which persons form part of the participant's present social network;
- How close these persons are to the participant relative to the other persons that figure on the sociogram;
- The nature and quality of the relationships that are depicted;

- The kind of influence these persons (or clusters of persons) have on the participant.

In the first session of this step, the sociogram is explained to the participants.

B: Assignment

The participants are asked to draw their own sociograms.

The sociogram of each participant is then discussed and the following questions are answered:

1. How does your present social network influence your thoughts and opinions?
2. How does your present social network influence your emotions?
3. How does your present social network influence your use of alcohol and/or drugs?
4. How does your present social network influence your criminal behavior?
5. Which persons or groups of persons influence you the most and in what way?
6. Which persons or groups of persons are good for you and which are bad or “toxic” for you?
7. If your social network would stay unchanged for the next ten years, what would your life be like?
8. If your social network would stay unchanged for the next ten years, what would you be like?
9. What would you like to change about your social network?

The answers to these questions and other relevant observations are written down in the workbook.

C: Homework

For homework, the participants are asked to reflect on their sociograms and to write down in their workbooks any relevant thoughts they may have concerning their social networks. They may adjust or completely redraw their sociograms when deemed appropriate. This homework will be discussed at the beginning of the next session.

STEP 3: THE ENHANCEMENT OF THE ABILITY TO RECOGNIZE PROSOCIAL PEOPLE AND TO DESIGNATE FINDING PLACES OF PROSOCIAL PEOPLE

A: Synopsis

In this step, there are two key questions:

1. Who are these prosocial people?
2. Where can I find these people?

The answers to these questions will vary from person to person and from culture to culture. However, there are some universal characteristics of prosocial people that can be used as starting points for seeking the answers to these questions.

- Prosocial people are neither superheroes nor saints. They are not perfect and they do make mistakes from time to time just like everybody else.
- Prosocial people are not (necessarily) dull and square. There are all kinds of prosocial people. They may be modern or traditional, conformist or critical towards society. They may have many different personal styles and walks of life. Prosocial people are very diverse; they do not meet a fixed description.
- Prosocial people care about others. They are empathic. They respect others and their opinions. They help people who need help. They like sharing what they have with others. They are careful about not betraying your trust.
- Prosocial people make something positive of their lives. They do not abuse alcohol or drugs. They are not involved in crime or injustice. They strive to be meaningful to others and to themselves.

After discussing the two questions, the next assignments are given:

B: Assignments

Assignment 1

The participants are asked to make a list of five prosocial people they know. Behind each name they write:

- Why this person is prosocial;
- What this person does in life;
- A description of his/her personality and lifestyle;
- Whether or not the participant would like to become friends with this person, and why this is so.

When the participants have completed their lists, they will discuss what kind of prosocial people they would prefer to get acquainted with. All new insights, conclusions and advices are written down in the workbook.

Assignment 2

According to the so-called "Law of Attraction," like attracts like. This means that prosocial people often tend to come together in certain places. This goes not only for the fact that they are prosocial, they also tend to group together in places where they can share things they have a passion for, like their taste in music, their faith, their hobby, their favorite sport, etc. These places are the designated finding places of prosocial people. These finding places will differ from one participant to another since different people have different preferences.

In the previous assignment, the participants have determined what kind of prosocial people they would prefer to get to know and be friends with. In this assignment they are asked to make a list of places where these prosocial people are often present. Usually, good places to find all kinds of prosocial people are places where volunteer work is done.

Behind each finding place on the list, the participant writes down whether or not he/she would feel comfortable to go there and why this is so.

The list of finding places is then discussed and additional finding places are suggested. Again, all new insights, conclusions, and advices are written down in the workbook.

C: Homework

In this step, the homework consists of the critical reflection on the assignments completed during the sessions.

Step 4: The Enhancement of Motivation in the Participant to Develop a Prosocial Network by Creating Awareness of the Advantages of Being Part of Such a Social Network

A: Synopsis

During the first session of this step, it is explained again to the participants that one of the most important protective factors against relapse and criminal recidivism is being part of a prosocial network. The characteristics of prosocial people as they were defined in steps 1 and 3 are recapitulated. It is also explained that people suffering from an addiction who have a criminal history, once having developed a prosocial network, are more successful in:

- Controlling their addiction,
- Staying out of trouble with the law,
- Work and income,
- Friendships and intimate relationships,
- Finding purpose in life,
- Developing new skills and interests,
- Attaining a higher quality of life in general.

B: Assignments

Assignment 1

In the first assignment of this step, the participants discuss their ideas about what their lives would be like if they would be part of a prosocial network.

During this discussion, the following questions are answered:

1. How would my life be different from what it is now?
2. Would I still be abusing substances? Why or why not?
3. Would I still be committing crimes? Why or why not?
4. Would I be happier? Why or why not?
5. What would I be doing in life/with my life?
6. Would I be richer/wealthier?

Of course, other relevant questions can be added to this list.
The participants will write down their answers in their workbooks.

Assignment 2

In the second assignment of this step, the participants are given the following list of statements that are typical of prosocial persons:

- I think it is important to help other people.
- I like to solve conflicts without hurting others.
- I like to tell the truth, even when this is not easy.
- I like to take part in activities that make my living environment/neighborhood a better place to live in.
- I am sensitive to the problems and needs of others.
- I respect other people, no matter who they are.
- I respect other people's views and opinions, even if they are opposite to (or very different from) those of my own.
- I know the difference between assertiveness and aggression and I definitely prefer assertiveness.

If desired, other such statements can be added to this list.
The participants then discuss these statements and answer the following questions:

1. Which of these statements appeal to you? Why?
2. Which of these statements don't appeal to you? Why?
3. What is respect? How do you define it? Are there other definitions of the word "respect"?
4. In which ways could you help other people? Which skills do you have or would you like to acquire?

5. In which ways could you contribute to the improvement of your living environment/neighborhood? Which skills do you have or would you like to acquire?

The participants will write their answers to these questions in their workbooks.

Assignment 3

In this assignment, the participants are provided with a balance sheet in which they take stock of their reasons for and against reforming their social network. When the balance sheets are completed, the participants discuss all the pros and contras. Concluding this assignment, every participant takes a decision about whether or not to reform his or her social network. Participants who have reached a firm conclusion not to reform their social network will leave the program.

C: Homework

In this step, the homework consists of the critical reflection on the assignments completed during the sessions.

STEP 5: THE DESIGN OF A PROSOCIAL NETWORK THAT MATCHES THE PARTICIPANT'S PERSONALITY, NEEDS, AND PREFERENCES

A: Synopsis

In this step, the participants design their ideal prosocial network. This is done by:

1. Determining which persons should be excluded from the participant's present social network,
2. Determining which persons should be included in the participant's future social network, and
3. Determining which persons should stay in the participant's social network. It should also be determined in what way the participant's

relationship to these persons should change in order to enhance the participant's quality of life and to reduce the risk of relapse and re-offending.

B: Assignments

Assignment 1

In this assignment, the participants take the sociogram they have drawn in step 2 and make the following changes:

1. The individuals who should be excluded from the participant's social network are marked with a red circle. The reasons why these individuals should be parted with are written down next to the sociogram.
2. The individuals about whom there is doubt whether or not they should be excluded from the participant's social network are marked with a yellow circle. The reasons for this doubt are written down next to the sociogram.
3. The individuals who should stay in the participant's social network are marked with a green circle. The reasons why these individuals should stay are written down next to the sociogram.

This new version of the sociogram is then discussed. Special attention is given to the individuals inside the participants' social networks about whom doubt exists whether or not they should be excluded. By considering all pros and contras, the participants finally decide on whether or not to exclude these individuals from their social networks.

Assignment 2

In the second assignment of this step, the participants are encouraged to fantasize about their future prosocial network and about what type of persons would make part of it. After a free discussion about the desired characteristics of future prosocial friends, each participant makes an inventory of one's own preferred characteristics which is written down in the workbook. After this, fictional characters are invented that possess these characteristics. These characters are named and provided with a fictional life story, a description of occupations and favorite pastimes, a list of places they frequent, etc. It is also allowed to include existing persons into this fantasy who are known to possess the desired characteristics. Finally, a new sociogram is drawn in the workbook in which these fictional characters and real people, together with the already existing prosocial relationships, are placed according to the preferences of the participant. This sociogram is then discussed as to its hypothetical effects on the participant's future life and as to the degree of attainability of such a social network. Adjustments to the sociogram are then made if necessary. The final version of this sociogram could be regarded as the participant's "ideal sociogram."

Assignment 3

In this assignment, the participants are encouraged to reflect about what they should do in order to improve their relationships with significant prosocial others in their present social network. First of all, the participants make a list of the people inside their present social network who have a positive influence on them. After this, they write down behind the name of each person what the current status of the relationship is and which problems are to be solved within these relationships. The possible solutions to these problems are then discussed, as well as the concrete actions each participant should undertake in order to bring improvement to their positive relationships. All conclusions and advices that result from this discussion are written down by the participant in his or her workbook.

C: Homework

In this step, the homework consists of the critical reflection on the assignments completed during the sessions.

Step 6: The Exploration of the Participant's Own Possibilities and Skills to Develop a Rewarding Prosocial Network

A: Synopsis

In this step, the participants will explore their already existing possibilities, capabilities, and skills to develop a prosocial network.

It is crucial in this step to make the participants focus on whatever possibilities, capabilities, and skills they have and not to dwell on any of their perceived shortcomings. Motivating the participants by enhancing their self-esteem is the main goal of this step. An improved self-esteem is important for the participants in order to gain confidence of the fact that they can be accepted in circles of prosocial people.

B: Assignment

The participants are asked to write down their strong points in the following areas:

- Character and personality;
- Practical and occupational skills;
- Social skills;
- Other fields of competence.

These strong points will be discussed as to how they can be used for the development of a prosocial network. All conclusions and advices that result from this discussion are written down by the participant in his or her workbook.

C: Homework

In this step, the homework consists of the critical reflection on the notes that were taken during the sessions.

Step 7: The Acquisition of Relevant Social Skills

A: Synopsis

In this step, the participants will inventory the social skills they lack in order to develop a prosocial network successfully as well as the possibilities that are available to them to enhance these skills. In most cases, this will involve taking part in a social skills training. All participants will receive information about what a social skills training is and where they can find such a training.

B: Assignment

The participants are asked to write down their weak points in the area of social skills. These weak points will be discussed as to how they can be turned into strong points as much as possible. All conclusions and advices that result from this discussion are written down by the participant in his or her workbook.

C: Homework

In this step, the homework consists of the critical reflection on the notes that were taken during the sessions and the careful consideration of whether or not to take part in a social skills training.

STEP 8: THE PREPARATION OF THE PARTICIPANT FOR THE BUDDY-ASSISTED PART OF THE PROGRAM

A: Synopsis

In this step, the participants are prepared for the second phase of the program in which they will start building up a prosocial network with the help of a buddy. This buddy is a volunteer who has been trained to adequately assist the participants to fulfill the goals of this program. The buddy will *not* become one of the participant's new prosocial friends. He or she will only encourage the participant and facilitate his or her efforts for the period of one year. The role of the buddy is to motivate and to accompany the participant while visiting the designated finding places and making contact with prosocial people. After this one-year period, the participant is considered to be able to maintain and expand his or her prosocial network without the assistance of a trained volunteer.

The assistance of a buddy in the second phase of the program is essential because most participants will experience high levels of discomfort when making their first steps into finding places of prosocial people. Without the support of a buddy, attrition can be expected to be high in this phase of the program.

A more detailed description of the recruitment, the role, and the training of the buddy is found further on in this chapter, in de paragraphs that describe phase two of this program.

B: Assignment

The participants are asked to discuss the following topics:

- How can a buddy help you to go to finding places of prosocial people?
- How can a buddy help you to make contact with prosocial people?
- How can a buddy help you to maintain a new prosocial friendship for at least one year?

All conclusions and advices that result from this discussion are written down in the participant's workbook.

C: Homework

In this step, the homework consists of the critical reflection on the notes that were taken during the sessions.

Step 9: Making a Prosocial Network Plan

A: Synopsis

In this last step of phase one, the participants will make their Prosocial Network Plan. This is a plan in which is determined:

1. Which ten finding places the participants will visit (together with their buddy). These finding places are written down in order of difficulty: the easiest first and the most difficult last. Each participant decides in

which order the finding places will be visited. A participant will move from one finding place to the next when at least one new prosocial acquaintance is made.

2. What the participants will do once they are at the finding place in order to meet prosocial people and get into contact with them, and how their buddy can help them to achieve this. Also a plan B is made in case plan A fails.
3. What the participants will do in order to develop (at least some of) these new acquaintances into durable friendships.
4. How the participants can check whether the new acquaintances are indeed prosocial. Also is determined how to end the relationship with newly met people that prove to be antisocial or "toxic."

The Prosocial Network Plan is the fundament of the second phase of the program. It serves as a "mission plan" for the first year of the development of the participant's prosocial network.

B: Assignment

Each participant draws up his or her own personal Prosocial Network Plan. The early versions of it are discussed and adjusted if necessary until a final version is formulated. The final version should be both realizable and agreeable to the participant. The final version of the Prosocial Network Plan is written down in the workbook.

C: Homework

In this step, the homework consists of the critical reflection on the Prosocial Network Plan until a final version is drafted.

PHASE 2, PUTTING THEORY INTO PRACTICE

The Buddy

Building up a prosocial network on one's own is simply too big a task for most participants. Therefore, each participant will carry out his or her

Prosocial Network Plan with the assistance and support of a buddy. As stated earlier, this buddy will stay with the participant for a period of one year. The buddy's role is:

- To accompany the participant to the finding places of prosocial people;
- To encourage the participant to carry out the planned actions at the finding places;
- To coach the participant while making contact with prosocial people;
- To support, motivate, and encourage the participant when he or she is being unsuccessful;
- To prevent postponement of action and attrition of the participant;
- To support, motivate, and encourage the participant not to resume contact with old criminogenic or "toxic" friends;
- To report the participant's progress to the therapists.

Not just anybody can become a buddy in this program. The buddy should:

- Be 25 years or older;
- Have an ample amount of social skills;
- Be assertive and steadfast;
- Not be involved in criminal or antisocial activities;
- Not have any problems with substances or gambling;
- Not have any (significant) psychological problems;
- Not be a fellow participant;
- Be a good match with the participant;
- Have a prosocial network himself/herself;
- Be a good motivator.

Usually, good places to recruit buddies are religious organizations (like churches, mosques, synagogues, The Salvation Army, etc.), and other organizations that have an idealistic and altruistic foundation (like environmental organizations, equal rights groups, volunteer organizations that support disadvantaged people, etc.). In many countries, there are numerous already existing buddy projects. Some of them may be willing to contribute to this program by recruiting specially selected buddies.

Preparation of the Buddy

Before entering the program, the buddy needs to be thoroughly informed about the program and its goals, and about the characteristics of its participants. The buddy must be made conscious of the fact that the person he or she will be helping to build up a prosocial network has a criminal history and a substance abuse problem. Therefore, each candidate should follow a preparation course in which the following topics are discussed:

- The characteristics of people suffering from SUDs;
- The characteristics of addicted delinquents;
- The influences and effects of an antisocial and a prosocial network;
- How the program works;
- The role of the buddy: what the buddy does and must not do;
- Personal safety issues which may arise from the relation with the participant.

It is only after having followed this preparation course that the candidate will decide whether or not to proceed with becoming a buddy.

Safety of the Buddy

Being the buddy of an addicted person who has a criminal history brings about personal safety issues. Therefore, a tailor-made safety plan is drawn up for each participant-buddy combination. This plan includes:

1. An inventory of the signals that can be regarded as precursors of situations of unsafety for the buddy.
2. A description of what the buddy should and should not do when these signals are observed;
3. Who to call for assistance when these signals are observed.

The buddy will always have his or her mobile phone at hand while undertaking activities with the participant.

The buddy's activities within the program will be discontinued in whatever case his or her personal safety is compromised by the participant.

Matching the Buddy with the Participant

Once the buddies are prepared for their role and activities, the therapists will match them to the participants with whom they believe they will form the best combination. Matching factors to take into consideration are age, sex, cultural background, tastes, preferences, dressing style, but especially character.

The therapists will introduce the participant to the buddy and organize three meetings of an hour in which the participant and the buddy can get to know each other and can determine whether or not they can form a good team together. If the participant and the buddy both agree to proceed together, they will. If at least one of them has doubts after these three meetings, the match is off and the buddy and the participant will be matched with someone else.

When a match is made, another meeting will be organized in which the participant's Prosocial Network Plan is discussed, as well as the buddy's personal safety plan. They will both sign a contract which states that:

1. In case of crises of calamities of any kind, the participant *will not* call upon the buddy for help. Rather, the participant will call upon professional caregivers for help and assistance.
2. The buddy will *never* lend or give any money or goods to the participant. The participant will *never* ask the buddy for money or goods.
3. The participant will *never* enter or come near the buddy's home while participating in the program. The participant will always respect the buddy's privacy. The participant will never ask de buddy for shelter. When shelter is needed, the participant will turn to professional care providers.
4. The participant and the buddy will not engage in any kind of sexual activity with each other for the duration of the program.
5. The buddy will *never* be under the influence of *any* substance while in the presence of the participant.
6. The buddy will *never* supply the participant with *any* addictive substance.
7. The buddy will *never* undertake *any* unlawful activity together with the participant.
8. The participant will *never* introduce the buddy to members of his or her criminogenic social network. The participant and the buddy will

never go to places where these people are present. The buddy will never associate with these people.

9. Both participant and buddy will abide by the Prosocial Network Plan and the buddy's personal safety plan. Any changes to any of the plans should be discussed with, and approved by the therapists first.
10. Both participant and buddy will contact one the therapists at least once a week and report truthfully on the progress, mishaps, and any other facts that can be reasonably considered as relevant.

Breaching this contract will usually mean the termination of the program for both participant and buddy.

The Participant-Buddy-Therapist Triangle

It is essential that the participant, the buddy and the therapist work closely together during the course of the program. The "triangle" will meet at least once a week to discuss progress, problems, and solutions to problems. Once every six weeks, the Prosocial Network Plan is evaluated and adjusted if necessary. The therapist provides coaching to both participant and buddy.

Ending the Program

The program ends when:

- The goals of the program are reached.
- The buddy's personal safety or well-being is compromised by the participant or by the program.
- The program proves to be counterproductive for the participant in any way.
- The contract between the participant and the buddy has been breached.

Conclusion

Since a number of years, Beating the Scene is successfully used by several forensic treatment clinics in the Netherlands. It has a high degree of acceptance in both participants and health care professionals. Although empirical research as to its efficacy is still due to take place, a clear consensus exists among the professionals who work with this intervention that it significantly contributes to the prevention of criminal recidivism and relapse to substance use. Most participants report that this intervention has helped them to attain a better quality of life, not only in terms of the acquisition of new meaningful relationships, but also in terms of the finding of purpose in their lives.

The intervention as described here can be used "as is," or it can be modified to be compatible with different cultures, subcultures and personal situations and characteristics. It can also be used in non-forensic treatment centers with patients who do not display any form of criminal behavior. For this purpose, all elements that are related to delinquency can simply be omitted.

References

Andrews, D. A., Bonta, J., and Hoge, R. D. (1990). Classification for effective rehabilitation: Rediscovering psychology. *Criminal Justice and Behavior*, 17, 19-52.

Andrews, D. A., and Bonta, J. (2006). *The psychology of criminal conduct* (4th ed.). Newark, NJ: LexisNexis.

Andrews, D. A., Bonta, J., and Wormith, S. J. (2006). The recent past and near future of risk and/or need assessment. *Crime and Delinquency*, 52, 7-27.

Beattie, M.C., and Longabaugh, R. (1999). General and alcohol-specific social support following treatment. *Addictive Behaviors*, 24, Issue 5, September-October, 593-606.

Berg, M.T., and Huebner, B.M. (2011). Reentry and the Ties that Bind: An Examination of Social Ties, Employment, and Recidivism. *Justice Quarterly*, 28, Issue 2, 382-410.

Bonta, J., and Andrews, D.A. (2007). *Risk-Need-Responsivity Model for Offender Assessment and Rehabilitation. Report 2007-06.* Public Safety Canada.

Brewer, D.D., Catalano, R.F., Haggerty, K., Grainey, R.R., and Fleming, C.B. (1998). Research Report: A meta-analysis of predictors of continued drug use during and after treatment for opiate addiction. *Addiction*, 93, 73-92.

Dobkin, P.L., De Civita, M., Paraherakis, A., and Gill, K. (2002). The role of functional social support in treatment retention and outcomes among outpatient adult substance abusers. *Addiction*, 97, Issue 3, pages 347-356.

Ennett, S.T., Bauman, K.E., Hussong, A., Faris, R., Foshee, V.A., Cai, L., and DuRant, R.H. (2006). The Peer Context of Adolescent Substance Use: Findings from Social Network Analysis. *Journal of Research on Adolescence*, 16, Issue 2, 159-186.

Hipp, J.R., Petersilia, J., and Turner, S. (2010). Parolee Recidivism in California: The effect of neighborhood context and social service agency characteristics. *Criminology*, 48, Issue 4, 947-979.

Levy, M.S. (2008). Listening to Our Clients: The Prevention of Relapse. *Journal of Psychoactive Drugs*, 40, Issue 2, 167-172.

Marlatt, G.A., and Witkiewitz, K. (2005). Relapse Prevention for Alcohol a nd Drug Problems. In: Marlatt, G.A., and Donovan, D.M. (Eds.) *Relapse Prevention, Maintenance strategies in the treatment of addictive behaviors.* Second Edition, 1-14. New York: The Guilford Press.

McIntosh, J., and McKeganey, N. (2000). The Recovery from Dependent Drug Use: addicts' strategies for reducing the risk of relapse. *Drugs: Education, Prevention and Policy*, 7, Issue 2, 179-192.

Miller, W.R., and Rollnick, S. (2002). "*Motivational Interviewing: Preparing People to Change.*" New York, NY: Guilford Press.

Moreno, J. L. (1934). *Who Shall Survive*?, New York, NY: Beacon House

Pearson, M., and Michell, L. (2000). Smoke Rings: social network analysis of friendship groups, smoking and drug-taking. Drugs: *Education, Prevention and Policy*, 7, Issue 1, 21-37.

Rachlin, H. (2000). The Lonely Addict. In: Bickel, W.K., and Vuchinich, R.E. (Eds.) *Reframing Health Behavior Change With Behavioral Economics.* Mahwah, NJ: Lawrence Erlbaum Associates Publishers.

Russel, J., and Cohn, R. (2015). *Sociogram.* Miami, FL: Book on Demand.

Skog, O.J. (2003). Addiction: Definitions and Mechanisms. In: Vuchinich, R.E., and Heather, N. (Eds.) *Choice, Behavioral Economics and Addiction.* Boston MA: Pergamon.

Tate, S.R., Brown, S.A., Unrod, M., and Ramo, R.E. (2004). Context of relapse for substance-dependent adults with and without comorbid psychiatric disorders. *Addictive Behaviors*, 29, Issue 9, December, 1707-1724.

Ward, T., and Gannon, T. (2006). Rehabilitation, etiology, and self-regulation: The Good Lives Model of sexual offender treatment. *Aggression and Violent Behavior*, 11, 77-94.

Ward, T., and Marshall, W.L. (2004). Good lives, etiology, and the rehabilitation of sex offenders: A bridging theory. *Journal of Sexual Aggression*, 10, 153-169.

In: Substance Abuse
Editor: Tanya Reid

ISBN: 978-1-63485-612-6

Chapter 6

EPIDEMIOLOGY OF HEPATITIS B VIRUS INFECTION AMONG NON-INJECTING DRUG USERS IN THE STATE OF PARÁ, BRAZILIAN AMAZON

Izadora R. Gaspar[1], Maria J. O. Magalhães[1], Viviane A. Sousa[1], Jairo A. A. Castro[2], Carlos E. M. Amaral[2], Renata B. Hermes[2], Marcelo L. Pinheiro[3], Luciana M. C. Maradei-Pereira[2], José Alexandre R. Lemos[3] and Aldemir B. Oliveira-Filho[1*]

[1]Institute for Coastal Studies, Federal University of Pará, Bragança PA, Brazil
[2]Center for Hemotherapy and Hematology of Pará, Belém PA, Brazil
[3]Institute for Biological Sciences, Federal University of Pará, Belém PA, Brazil

---

* Corresponding Author: Aldemir B. Oliveira-Filho. Faculty of Natural Sciences, Institute for Coastal Studies, Campus of Bragança, Federal University of Pará (UFPA), Bragança PA, Brazil. Alameda Leandro Ribeiro, s/n. Aldeia. 68.600-000. Bragança, Pará, Brazil. Phone: + 55 91 3425 1209. E-mail: olivfilho@ufpa.br.

ABSTRACT

Hepatitis B virus (HBV) is a major cause of cirrhosis and hepatocellular carcinoma, even after introduction of vaccination programs in recent decades. Brazil is considered an area of low prevalence of HBV infections, however has record of high prevalence of HBV infections in locations in the Brazilian Amazon. To date, few epidemiological studies have been conducted on vulnerable populations in the Amazon. This study determined the prevalence and factors associated with HBV infection among non-injecting drug users in the state of Pará, Brazilian Amazon. This was a cross-sectional study conducted in private and public drug-treatment centers in nine municipalities in the state of Pará, Brazilian Amazon. All non-injecting drug users provided information through face-to-face interview. The diagnosis of HBV infection was obtained by EIA and real-time PCR. Simple and multiple logistic regressions were done to assess the risk factors associated with HBV infection. During 2008-2011, 300 non-injecting drug users attending drug-treatment centers participated in this study. Most non-injecting drug users were male (63.7%). The mean age was 32.5 years. The non-injecting drugs most consumed were: crack cocaine, cannabis, and cocaine paste. Tobacco and alcohol were also commonly consumed. In total, 81 (27.0%) non-injecting drug users were exposed to HBV. Being that, 12 users had HBV-DNA. The genotype A (50.0%), D (33.3%) and F (16.7%) were identified. Several risk factors were associated with HBV infection: age ≥35 years, male, tattoos, use of drugs for more than five years, use of drugs everyday, unprotected sex, sexual intercourse with another drug user, involvement in prostitution, and more than 20 sexual partners over the past 2 years. This study identified relevant epidemiological information of HBV infection in non-injecting drug users. It determined a high prevalence of HBV infection, being detected predominance of genotype A. Possibly, the spread of HBV is associated with factors related sexual and parenteral routes and the time of life and drug use.

Keywords: HBV, epidemiology, non-injecting drug users, Amazon

INTRODUCTION

The hepatitis B virus (HBV) infection is an important public health problem around the world. There are an estimated 250 million HBV carriers in the world, from which nearly a million die annually from HBV associated

following variables were determined: gender, age, close family or friends with viral hepatitis, recipient of blood transfusion, had surgery during the subject's lifetime, had invasive dental treatment (root canal or tartar removal) during the subject's lifetime, tattoo, shared used of razor blades in the domestic environment, shared used of blades in a barbershop, beauty salon or similar environment, use of a needle or syringe sterilized at home, shared nail clippers, types of legal drugs used during the subject's lifetime, total time of drug use, frequency of drug use, shared use of drug paraphernalia (tubes, cans, pipes and similar), have already been arrested in police station or prison, use of drugs during detention in jails or prison, sexual orientation,unprotected sex, sexual intercourse with another drug user, involvement in prostitution, andmultiple sexual partners.

Furthermore, DTC structured admission records were reviewed to assess drug-use histories. The records include data on drug preference, length of drug use, sexual risk behavior, the main drugs used and their routes of administration. When clients enter treatment, each major part of the body-head, trunk, extremities and so on is examined. If needle use indications are identified, they are recorded in the client's records. The information provided by participants through the questionnaire was compared with the records stored in DTC to identify and delete injecting drug users.

Confidence intervals were constructed for the infection prevalence estimates. Simple and multiple logistic regressions were done to assess the independent effect of variables [24]. The fit of the final model was assessed using the Hosmer-Lemeshow goodness-of-fit test. In statistical analysis, the HBV infection was defined by the presence of HBsAg antigen and/or presence of anti-HBc antibodies. All statistical analyses were carried out using IBM SPSS Statistics version 18.0.

RESULTS

In total, 327 illicit drug users agreed to participate in the study. However, twenty-seven patients had records of injection drug use and were excluded from analysis. According to information provided by 300 non-injecting drug users, this epidemiological study was developed. Most non-injecting drug users were male (63.7%). The mean age was 32.5 ± 10.3 years (median = 31 years). None of non-injecting drug users considered themselves to be ex-drug users (patients who reported that if they left drug-treatment centers (DTC) at the time of the interview, they would not resume using illicit drugs). Several participants (49.1%) reported having consumed more than one illicit drug during their lifetime. Thus, illicit-drug users were grouped according to the drug used most frequently. Drug preference was grouped into seven categories: crack cocaine (36.7%), cannabis (15.6%), cocaine paste (21.3%), cannabis + cocaine paste (11.7%), cocaine powder (14.0%), and cocaine powder + paste (0.7%). Tobacco (60.9%) and alcohol (79.4%) were also commonly consumed by the subjects.

In 300 non-injecting drug users, 81 (27.0%) were exposed to HBV. Among which, three (1.0%) users had positive results only for HBsAg, five (2.7%) for HBsAg + anti-HBc, and 50 (16.7%) for anti-HBc + anti-HBs. In addition, 23 (7.7%) users had positive results only for anti-HBc. Six (2.0%) users had positive results only for anti-HBs, suggesting that they were vaccinated and have not been exposed to HBV. Among users exposed to HBV, 22 (27.2%) users presented positive results for anti-HIV antibodies and 10 (12.3%) users presented positive results for anti-HCV antibodies (Table 1).

All non-injecting drug users with positive results for HBsAg also had positive results for HBV-DNA. One user with positive result for anti-HBc, and three users with positive results for anti-HBc + anti-HBs were detected HBV-DNA. The positivity of these four samples was confirmed by the repetition of isolation and amplification of viral DNA. Thus, the prevalence of occult HBV infection was 5.5% (4/73) among patients with positive results for anti-HBc. The HBV genotypes were identified in 12 non-injecting drug users with positive results for HBsAg and anti-HBc. Based on real-time PCR, genotype A (n = 6; 50.0%), D (n = 4, 33.3%) and F (n = 2; 16.7%) were identified.

Table 1. Prevalence of serological markers for HBV, HCV and HIV among non-injecting drug users in the state of Pará, Brazilian Amazon

Serological markers	Positive		CI 95%
	N	%	
HBV			
HBsAg	3	1.0	0.0 - 3.8
Anti-HBc	23	7.7	3.2 - 12.4
HBsAg + Anti-HBc	5	2.7	0.0 - 6.3
Anti-HBc + anti-HBs	50	16.7	10.6 - 22.3
Some exposition marker	81	27.0	22.9 - 32.3
Anti-HBs	6	2.0	0.0 - 5.7
HCV			
Anti-HCV*	10	12.3	8.2 - 16.3
HIV			
Anti-HIV*	22	27.2	23.9 - 30.7

* Results of tests performed with 81 non-injecting drug users exposed to HBV.

Table 2. Socio-demographic and epidemiological characteristics associated to HBV seropositivity among non-injecting drug users in the state of Pará, Brazilian Amazon

Characteristics	*N* (%)	*n* HBV+ (%)	OR (CI 95%)
Total	300	81 (27.0)	-
Mean age (years)	32.5	36.0	
Age ≥ 35 years	114 (38.0)	60 (74.1)	8.7 (4.9 - 15.7)
Male	191 (63.7)	62 (76.5)	2.3 (1.3 - 4.1)
Homosexual + Bisexual	21 (7.0)	9 (11.1)	2.1 (0.8 - 5.3)
Possible routes of HBV infection			
Family member or friend with viral hepatitis	23 (7.7)	8 (9.9)	1.5 (0.6 - 3.7)
Recipient of blood transfusion	40 (13.3)	14 (17.3)	1.6 (0.8 - 3.1)
Surgery	139 (46.3)	41 (4.9)	1.3 (0.7 - 2.1)
Tattoos	177 (59.0)	69 (85.2)	5.9 (3.0 - 11.5)
Shared used of razor blades in the domestic environment	102 (34.0)	31 (38.3)	1.3 (0.7 - 2.2)
Shared used of blades in a barbershop/beauty salon	81 (27.0)	20 (24.7)	0.8 (0.4 - 1.5)
Use of needle or sterilized glass syringe at home	72 (24.0)	23 (28.4)	1.4 (0.8 - 2.5)
Sharing nail clippers	130 (43.3)	45 (55.6)	1.0 (0.6 - 1.7)
Invasive dental treatment	227 (75.7)	55 (67.9)	0.6 (0.3 - 1.0)
Shared use of drug paraphernalia	204 (68.0)	60 (74.1)	1.5 (0.8 - 2.6)
Use of drugs for more than five years	199 (66.3)	71 (87.7)	5.0 (2.5 - 10.3)
Use of drugs everyday	246 (82.0)	70 (86.4)	2.9 (1.2 - 6.7)
Have already been arrested in police station or prison	84 (28.0)	29 (25.8)	1.7 (0.9 - 2.9)
Unprotected sex	234 (78.0)	76 (93.8)	5.9 (2.3 - 15.2)
Sexual intercourse with another drug user	191 (65.7)	73 (90.1)	7.8 (3.6 - 16.9)
Involvement in prostitution	157 (52.3)	60 (74.1)	3.6 (2.1 - 6.3)
More than 20 sexual partners over the past 24 months	138 (46.0)	65 (80.2)	8.2 (4.4 - 15.1)

Table 3. Risk factors for HBV infection by multiple logistic regression

Risk factors	*p-value*	*aOR* (CI 95%)
Male	0.03	2.0 (1.3 - 3.5)
Age ≥ 35 years	<0.01	8.5 (4.3 - 15.1)
Tattoos	0.01	5.5 (2.8 - 12.3)
Use of drugs for more than five years	0.01	5.3 (2.9 - 11.5)
Use of drugs everyday	0.03	2.4 (1.3 - 6.4)
Unprotected sex	<0.01	6.6 (2.5 - 16.1)
Sexual intercourse with another drug user	<0.01	8.1 (2.7 - 15.3)
Involvement in prostitution	0.02	3.2 (2.0 - 6.8)
More than 20 sexual partners over the past 24 months	<0.01	7.9 (3.8 - 15.6)

In Table 2, the results of the univariate analysis of potential risk factors for exposure to HBV are presented. Nine risk factors were associated with HBV infection: age ≥35 years, male, tattoos, use of drugs for more than five years, use of drugs everyday, unprotected sex, sexual intercourse with another drug user, involvement in prostitution, and more than 20 sexual partners over the past 2 years. In multivariate analysis, the same nine variables, identified by simple logistic regression were also indicated as risk factors for HBV infection, taking into account possible confounding variables (Table 3). The Hosmer-Lemeshow goodness-of-fit test showed a good fit for the final model ($HL\chi^2 = 12.2$; $p = 0.2$). Thus, this study showed that HBV transmission occurs through a network of factors involving sexual and parenteral routes linked to the user's age and time of use of illicit drugs.

DISCUSSION

In Brazil, there is a wide variation in the prevalence of HBV infections according to geographical area. The Brazilian Amazon has areas with high or intermediate endemicity of HBV infections [1, 7, 10]. The prevalence of HBV infections in this study was higher than that observed in studies conducted among users of illicit drugs in the Midwest (14.0%) and Southeast (12.9%) of Brazil [2, 11], being relatively similar to that observed in individuals from the Testing Center and counseling for AIDS and sexually transmitted infections (41.0%) in Pará [1].

Moreover, the prevalence of HCV and HIV infections in individuals exposed to HBV was much higher than those reported in blood donors (0.5% and 0.8%, respectively) and similar to those observed in users of illicit drugs in the state of Pará, Brazilian Amazon [8, 23, 25, 26, 28]. The prevalence of anti-HIV antibodies detected in this study is worrisome. Both HIV and HBV infections are mainly related to sexual transmission [11, 17, 27, 33]. Actions for prevention and control should be employed by health authorities to contain the spread of many sexually transmitted infections, including infections with HBV and HIV. Likely, an epidemiological research on HIV infection in users of illicit drugs in the state of Pará will occur in the future.

This study also provided information on the prevalence of occult HBV infection. Among 73 non-injecting drug users with negative results for HBsAg, 7 (9.6%) presented positive results for anti-HBc or anti-HBc + anti-HBs, and also positive results for HBV-DNA. Knowing that all the participants used non-injection drugs, the prevalence of occult HBV infection was relatively higher or similar to that observed in some epidemiological studies in Brazil. In Midwest, it has been detected prevalence of occult HBV infection around 2.7% (in non-injecting drug users) and 12.7% (in injecting drug users) [11, 19]. Moreover, the prevalence of occult HBV infection detected among injecting drug users in Argentina (7.7%), Taiwan (41.1%) and the United States (45.0%) are higher than observed in this study [16, 36, 38] According to Matos et al. [19], local endemicity patterns and methodological differences between the studies may lead to these differences in the prevalence of occult HBV infection in populations.

The HBV genotypes were identified in all samples diagnosed positive for HBV-DNA. Three different genotypes were found: A (50.0%), D (33.3%) and F (16.7%). These genotypes have been detected in other populations in Brazil, even among illicit drug users [10, 11, 20, 27, 32]. This distribution of HBV genotypes confirms the results of studies in other populations of the Brazilian Amazon [9, 20].

In regard to risk factors for HBV infection, this study indicated a network behaviors and epidemiological factors that have facilitated the spread of HBV among users of illicit drugs. As observed in other studies, the age may be associated with HBV infection due to increase of the cumulative risk of exposure to HBV through time, whether through sexual intercourse or parenterally [27, 30]. It was also observed an association of HBV infection with males. As described in other studies, possibly, this is a reflection of the more frequent exposure to factors related to the spread of HBV, particularly unprotected intercourse, engagement in prostitution and a high number of sexual partners, including other drug users [11, 19, 27, 31, 33].

In addition, this study indicated that tattoos is associated with HBV infection among non-injecting drug users. In Brazil, specifically among non-injecting drug users in the state of Pará, tattoos is commonly associated with the spread of HBV and HCV infection [25, 26, 27, 28]. The use of illicit drugs for a long time (more than three years) was also associated with HBV infection in this study. Other studies have also reported extensive use of illegal drugs as a risk factor for HBV infection [19, 25, 31, 33].

The present study has limitations that should be considered in the interpretation of results. No procedures for identifying injection drug use, including those used in this study, are foolproof. The number of non-injecting drug users and their general characteristics in the state of Pará are not actually known since drug use is an illicit activity. For that reason, HBV infection was only investigated among those non-injecting drug users enrolled in private and public drug treatment centers during the study period. On the other hand, given the scarcity of epidemiological data about HCV infection among illicit-drug users in the state do Pará, our results provide background infor- mation for formulating policies and strategies for reducing risk and damage associated to the use of illicit drugs.

Conclusion

This study identified relevant epidemiological information of HBV infection in non-injecting drug users. It determined a high prevalence of HBV infection among non-injecting drug users in Pará, being detected predominance of genotype A. Nine risk factors were associated with HBV infection, indicating that the spread of HBV is associated with factors related sexual and parenteral routes and the time of life and drug use.

Acknowledgments

Thanks to Leila Sawada (Tokyo Medical and Dental University, Japan), Laine C. Pinto (Federal University of Pará, Brazil), Daiane Locks (Federal University of Pará, Brazil), and Igor Brasil-Costa (Institute Evandro Chagas, Brazil) for the collaboration in information collection and database assembly. This study was supported by Secretariat of Health Surveillance (Ministry of Health, Brazil), and National Council for Scientific and Technological Development (Ministry of Science, Technology and Innovation, Brazil).

Competing interests: The authors declare that they have no competing interests.

References

[1] Aquino, J.A., Pegado, K.A., Barros, L.P., Machado, L.F. (2008). Seroprevalence of hepatitis B virus and hepatitis C virus infections among individuals in the State of Pará. *Rev Soc Bras Med Trop.* 41: 334-337.

[2] Bastos, F.I., Lowndes, C.M., Castello-Branco, L.R., Linhares-de-Carvalho, M.I., Oelemann, W., Bernier, F., Morgado, M.G., Yoshida,

C.F., Rozental, T., Alary, M. (2000). Sexual behaviour and infection rates for HIV, blood-borne and sexually transmitted infections among patients attending drug treatment centres in Rio de Janeiro, Brazil. *Int J STD AIDS*. 11: 383-392.

[3] Benzaken, A., Sabidó, M., Galban, E., Rodrigues Dutra, D.L., Leturiondo, A.L., Mayaud, P. (2012). HIV and sexually transmitted infections at the borderlands: situational analysis of sexual health in the Brazilian Amazon. *Sex Transm Infect*. 88: 294-300.

[4] Benzaken, A.S., Galbán Garcia, E., Sardinha, J.C., Pedrosa, V.L., Paiva, V (2007). Community-based intervention to control STD/AIDS in the Amazon region, Brazil. *Rev Saude Publica*. 41: S118-S126.

[5] Braga, W.S., Castilho, Mda C., Borges, F.G., Martinho, A.C., Rodrigues, I.S., Azevedo, E.P., Scazufca, M., Menezes, P.R. (2012). Prevalence of hepatitis B virus infection and carriage after nineteen years of vaccination program in the Western Brazilian Amazon. *Rev Soc Bras Med Trop*. 45: 13-17.

[6] Brasil, L.M., Fonseca, J.C.F., Souza, R.B., Braga, W.S.M., Toledo, L.M. (2003). Prevalence of hepatitis B virus markers within household contacts in the State of Amazonas. *Rev Soc Bras Med Trop*. 36: 565-570.

[7] Castilho, Mda C., Oliveira, C.M., Gimaque, J.B., Leão, J.D., Braga, W.S. (2012). Epidemiology and molecular characterization of hepatitis B virus infection in isolated villages in the Western Brazilian Amazon. *Am J Trop Med Hyg*. 87: 768-774.

[8] Costa, A.S.L., Brasiliense, D.M. (2011). HIV Seroconversion in blood donors from the coordinating blood bank in the State of Pará. *Rev Bras Hematol Hemoter*. 33: 342-346.

[9] Crispim, M.A., Fraiji, N.A., Campello, S.C., Schriefer, N.A., Stefani, M.M., Kiesslich D. (2014). Molecular epidemiology of hepatitis B and hepatitis delta viruses circulating in the Western Amazon region, North Brazil. *BMC Infect Dis*. 14: 94.

[10] De Almeida, M.K., Dos Santos, K.N., Fecury, A.A., De Oliveira, C.S., Freitas, A.S., Quaresma, J.A., Fuzii, H.T., Martins, L.C. (2012). Prevalence of viral hepatitis B and C in riverside communities of the Tucuruí Dam, Pará, Brazil. *J Med Virol*. 84: 1907-1912.

[11] Ferreira, R.C., Rodrigues, F.P., Teles, S.A., Lopes, C.L., Motta-Castro, A.R., Novais, A.C., Souto, F.J., Martins, R.M. (2009). Prevalence of hepatitis B virus and risk factors in Brazilian non-injecting drug users. *J Med Virol*. 81: 602-609.

[12] Franco, E., Bagnato, B., Marino, M.G., Meleleo, C., Serino, L., Zaratti, L. (2012). Hepatitis B: Epidemiology and prevention in developing countries. *World J Hepatol.* 4: 74-80.

[13] Kuo, I., Sherman, S.G., Thomas, D.L., Strathdee, S.A. (2004). Hepatitis B virus infection and vaccination among young injection and non-injection drug users: Missed opportunities to prevent infection. *Drug Alcohol Depend.* 73: 69-78.

[14] Lavanchy, D. (2005). Worldwide epidemiology of HBV infection, disease burden, and vaccine prevention. *J Clin Virol.* 34: S1-S3.

[15] Liaw, Y.F. (2009). Natural history of chronic hepatitis B virus infection and long-term outcome under treatment. *Liver Int.* 29: S100-S107.

[16] Lin, C.L., Liu, C.J., Chen, P.J., Lai, M.Y., Chen, D.S., Kao, J.H. (2007). High prevalence of occult hepatitis B virus infection in Taiwanese intravenous drug users. *J Med Virol.* 79: 1674-1678.

[17] Lum, P.J., Hahn, J.A., Shafer, K.P., Evans, J.L., Davidson, P.J., Stein, E., Moss, A.R. (2008). Hepatitis B virus infection and immunization status in a new generation of injection drug users in San Francisco. *J Viral Hepat.* 15: 229-236.

[18] Malmström, S., Berglin-Enquist, I., Lindh, M. (2010). Novel method for genotyping hepatitis B virus on the basis of TaqMan real-time PCR. *J Clin Microbiol.* 48: 1105-1111.

[19] Matos, M.A., Ferreira, R.C., Rodrigues, F.P., Marinho, T.A., Lopes, C.L., Novais, A.C., Motta-Castro, A.R., Teles, S.A., Souto, F.J., Martins, R.M. (2013). Occult hepatitis B virus infection among injecting drug users in the Central-West Region of Brazil. *Mem Inst Oswaldo Cruz.* 108: 383-385.

[20] Mello, F.C., Souto, F.J., Nabuco, L.C., Villela-Nogueira, C.A., Coelho, H.S., Franz, H.C., Saraiva, J.C., Virgolino, H.A., Motta-Castro, A.R., Melo, M.M., Martins, R.M., Gomes, S.A. (2007). Hepatitis B virus genotypes circulating in Brazil: molecular characterization of genotype F isolates. *BMC Microbiol.* 7:103.

[21] Nelson, N.P., Jamieson, D.J., Murphy, T.V. (2014).Prevention of Perinatal Hepatitis B Virus Transmission. *J Pediatric Infect Dis.* 3: S7-S12.

[22] Nelson, P.K., Mathers, B.M., Cowie, B., Hagan, H., Des Jarlais, D., Horyniak, D., Degenhardt, L. (2011). Global epidemiology of hepatitis B and hepatitis C in people who inject drugs: results of systematic reviews. *Lancet.* 378: 571-583.

[23] Oliveira-Filho, A.B., Pimenta, A.S., Rojas, M.F., Chagas, M.C., Crescente, J.A., Crespo, D.M., Lemos, J.A. (2010). Prevalence and genotyping of hepatitis C virus in blood donors in the state of Pará, Northern Brazil. *Mem Inst Oswaldo Cruz.* 105: 103-106.

[24] Oliveira-Filho, A.B., Pimenta, A.S., Rojas, M.F., Chagas, M.C., Crespo, D.M., Crescente, J.A., Lemos, J.A. (2010). Likely transmission of hepatitis C virus through sharing of cutting and perforating instruments in blood donors in the State of Pará, Northern Brazil. *Cad Saude Publica.* 26: 837-844.

[25] Oliveira-Filho, A.B., Sawada, L., Pinto, L.C., Locks, D., Bahia, S.L., Brasil-Costa, I., Lemos, J.A. (2013). HCV infection among cocaine users in the state of Pará, Brazilian Amazon. *Arch Virol.* 158: 1555-1560.

[26] Oliveira-Filho, A.B., Sawada, L., Pinto, L.C., Locks, D., Bahia, S.L., Castro, J.A., Hermes, R.B., Brasil-Costa, I., Amaral, C.E., Lemos, J.A. (2014). Epidemiological aspects of HCV infection in non-injecting drug users in the Brazilian state of Pará, eastern Amazon. *Virol J.* 11: 38.

[27] Oliveira, E.H., Lima-Verde, R.M., Pinheiro, L.M., Benchimol, M.G., Aragão, A.L., Lemos, J.A., Oliveira-Filho, A.B., Vallinoto, A.C. (2014). HBV infection in HIV-infected subjects in the state of Piauí, Northeast Brazil. *Arch Virol.* 159: 1193-1197.

[28] Pacheco, S.D., Silva-Oliveira, G.C., Maradei-Pereira, L.M., Crescente, J.A., Lemos, J.A., Oliveira-Filho, A.B. (2014). Prevalence of HCV infection and associated factors among illicit drug users in Breves, State of Pará, northern Brazil. *Rev Soc Bras Med Trop.* 47: 367-370.

[29] Paraná, R., Almeida, D. (2005). HBV epidemiology in Latin America. *J Clin Virol.* 34: S130-S133.

[30] Pereira, L.M., Martelli, C.M., Merchán-Hamann, E., Montarroyos, U.R., Braga, M.C., De Lima, M.L., Cardoso, M.R., Turchi, M.D., Costa, M.A., De Alencar, L.C., Moreira, R.C., Figueiredo, G.M., Ximenes, R.A. (2009). Hepatitis Study Group. Population-based multicentric survey of hepatitis B infection and risk factor differences among three regions in Brazil. *Am J Trop Med Hyg.* 81: 240-247.

[31] Reimer, J., Lorenzen, J., Baetz, B., Fischer, B., Rehm, J., Haasen, C., Backmund, M. (2007). Multiple viral hepatitis in injection drug users and associated risk factors. *J Gastroenterol Hepatol.* 22: 80-85.

[32] Ribeiro, N.R., Campos, G.S., Angelo, A.L., Braga, E.L., Santana, N., Gomes, M.M., Pinho, J.R., De Carvalho, W.A., Lyra, L.G., Lyra, A.C.

(2006). Distribution of hepatitis B virus genotypes among patients with chronic infection. *Liver Int.* 26: 636-642.

[33] Rich, J.D., Anderson, B.J., Schwartzapfel, B., Stein, M.D. (2006). Sexual risk for hepatitis B virus infection among hepatitis C virus-negative heroin and cocaine users. *Epidemiol Infect.* 134: 478-484.

[34] Shepard, C.W., Simard, E.P., Finelli, L., Fiore, A.E., Bell, B.P. (2006). Hepatitis B virus infection: epidemiology and vaccination. *Epidemiol Rev.* 28:112-125.

[35] Sitnik, R., Paes, A., Mangueira, C.P., Pinho, J.R. (2010). A real-time quantitative assay for hepatitis B DNA virus (HBV) developed to detect all HBV genotypes. *Rev Inst Med Trop Sao Paulo.* 52: 119-124.

[36] Torbenson, M., Kannangai, R., Astemborski, J., Strathdee, S.A., Vlahov, D., Thomas, D.L. (2004). High prevalence of occult hepatitis B in Baltimore injection drug users. *Hepatology.* 39: 51-57.

[37] Ucmak H, Faruk Kokoglu O, Celik M, Ergun UG (2007). Intra-familial spread of hepatitis B virus infection in eastern Turkey. *Epidemiol Infect.* 135: 1338-1343.

[38] Vitale, F., Tramuto, F., Orlando, A., Vizzini, G., Meli, V., Cerame, G., Mazzucco, W., Virdone, R., Palazzo, U., Villafrate, M.R., Tagger, A., Romano, N. (2008). Can the serological status of anti-HBc alone be considered a sentinel marker for detection of occult HBV infection? *J Med Virol.* 80: 577-582.

In: Substance Abuse
Editor: Tanya Reid

ISBN: 978-1-63485-612-6

Chapter 7

Exploring the Policy Context of Recovery High Schools: A Case Study of Schools in Minnesota and Massachusetts

Andrew J. Finch[1,*], Holly L. Karakos[2] and Emily A. Hennessy[1]
[1]Vanderbilt University, Nashville, Tennessee, US
[2]Equal Opportunity Schools, Seattle, Washington, US

Abstract

Communities provide a supportive ecology for adolescents in recovery; thus, it is illuminating to explore contextual influences that enable and/or hinder the emergence and sustainability of recovery high schools (RHS) – a recovery support for adolescents working to overcome addiction. In this article, we use ecological mapping to examine the developmental trajectory of RHS in two states where they have proliferated. Using these case studies, we discuss the macro- and micro-level factors that influence the emergence and sustainability of RHS and conclude that both grassroots advocates and policy-makers must consider

* Corresponding author: Andrew J. Finch, Human and Organizational Development, Vanderbilt University. Peabody College #90, 230 Appleton Place, Nashville, TN 37203, Email: andrew.j.finch@vanderbilt.edu.

the myriad ecological forces and their influence on the development of particular recovery support programs.

Keywords: adolescent, policy mapping, recovery high schools, substance use disorder

For individuals in recovery from substance use disorders (SUDs), supportive social contexts are exceedingly important in improving prospects for maintaining sobriety (e.g., Kelly & Urbanoski, 2012). Although supportive aftercare communities are important for most people in recovery, social support is especially important for *adolescents* in recovery as they must cope with the addiction itself while also rediscovering their role in their communities as a person in recovery, adding additional complexity to adolescents' already difficult task of identity development (Erikson, 1968). Communities are increasingly recognizing the need for tailored supports for adolescents returning from treatment (e.g., Fisher, 2014); yet, even with some recovery supports in place, rates of relapse are high (Burleson, Kaminer, & Burke, 2012). There is a need, therefore, for comprehensive, community-based recovery supports for adolescents.

One such community resource designed to provide comprehensive support to youth in recovery from SUDs is the recovery high school, or "sober school." Recovery high schools provide an intensive form of recovery support in one of the most salient developmental contexts for adolescents – school (Allison et al., 1999). Even as new recovery high schools continue to open throughout the country, however, their growth has been slow and punctuated by school closures. In order to understand the ways that communities provide a supportive ecology for adolescents in recovery, it is illuminating to understand the contextual influences that can either drive the development of or stifle recovery high schools. Thus, after describing recovery high schools, we use ecological mapping to examine the development of recovery high schools in two states. Based on these case studies, we discuss the macro- and micro-level factors that influence the emergence and sustainability of recovery high schools as a community resource for adolescents in recovery.

Recovery High Schools

There is a clear need for recovery supports for adolescents; approximately 8.4% of all substance abuse treatment admissions from 2000-2010 were for 12-17 year olds (Substance Abuse and Mental Health Administration [SAMHSA], 2012), and research consistently shows high rates of relapse among adolescents, with less than 50% remaining sober only three months after treatment (Brown et al., 2001; Burleson et al., 2012). Since their inception in 1979 (Finch, Moberg, & Krupp, 2014), there have been approximately 77 recovery high schools in existence, with about 36 currently in operation (Association of Recovery Schools, 2016). The schools were developed to provide youth with recovery-based educational support in a small school setting as an alternative to returning to their former schools where peers or other influences might trigger a relapse to substance use (Allison et al., 1999). Recovery high schools aim to reduce rates of relapse after treatment by providing a rigorous academic curriculum alongside recovery supports such as close student-teacher relationships, individual therapeutic sessions provided by licensed clinical or chemical health counselors, and group therapeutic sessions to strengthen sober peer supports (Karakos, 2014; Moberg, Finch, & Lindsley, 2014). Many schools also connect students with continuing care resources outside of the school, such as adolescent-friendly Alcoholics Anonymous (AA) or Narcotics Anonymous (NA) meetings.

Recent preliminary data (Finch et al., 2014; Finch, Moberg, Tanner-Smith, Karakos, 2014; Moberg, Finch, Winters, & Lipsey, 2013) and qualitative research (Kochanek, 2008; Moberg et al., 2014) support recovery high schools' effectiveness as recovery and academic environments for youth. For example, in one in-depth qualitative study of 17 recovery high schools in six U.S. states, students had significantly reduced their substance use and reported fewer instances of mental health symptoms since entering the school (Moberg & Finch, 2007). Additionally, 71% of students reported that they were doing better academically in the recovery school. As a result, United States Federal offices have recognized recovery schools as a viable support for adolescents post-treatment (Office of National Drug Control Policy, 2014; National Institute of Drug Abuse, 2014).

but there were also organizations (usually non-profits) formed expressly to operate an alternative school. Alternative schools who had contracts with public school districts in Minnesota are called "contract alternative schools." Today, there are also "district alternative schools," in which districts design and operate their own alternative schools, using district faculty, staff, and facilities (Farris-Berg & Schroeder, 2003, p. 6).

Alternative education programs were formally recognized by the state of Minnesota in 1987 with the passage of two "second chance laws" (Boyd, Hare, & Nathan, 2002). The first was the High School Graduation Incentives (HSGI) program that gave students at-risk of dropping out the option to transfer to programs that met their educational and/or social needs. The second law created Area Learning Centers (ALCs) to provide programs focusing on academics and workforce preparation. ALCs offer flexible programming, individualized instruction, specialized training, and work opportunities (Boyd et al., 2002). HSGI thus provided students with the legal mechanism for flexibility in their school choice, and ALCs provided options for students to choose from.

It is important to consider how these educational policies worked in unison. First, open enrollment made it possible for *all* students to choose schools *outside their resident district*, with per pupil funding following them. Second, the HSGI program ensured that students at-risk of dropping out would be able to choose among different school options. Finally, the creation of contract alternative schools and ALCs gave students access to schools designed specifically for individualized needs or workforce development, rather than a disciplinary alternative school program (Boyd et al., 2002); this provided school *options* for students having difficulties completing high school in their traditional public school. Without open enrollment, students would be restricted to schools in their zoned districts, and without the HSGI, students could have been excluded from choosing alternative schools. Minnesota's school choice policies created a fertile ground for recovery high schools, because SUDs were one of the qualifying conditions for being "at-risk" for dropping out under these statutes. Contract alternative schools and programs within the ALCs, thus, could be developed to target students with SUDs. In fact, almost all of the Minnesota recovery high schools were at one time a contract alternative school or part of an area learning center.

Charter Schools. In 1991, Minnesota became the first state to pass a charter school law that allowed groups of parents, educators, and community members to create new public schools independent of most state regulations (Laws of Minnesota, 1991). These schools were required to participate in statewide testing programs, had to be non-sectarian, and were not allowed to use admissions tests. Minnesota has continued its commitment to charter schools, and as of 2013, was deemed to have the second most amenable charter school laws in the nation (Center for Education Reform, 2013). The state now permits an unlimited number of charter schools to open, and one of the four recovery high schools in Minnesota is a charter school.

Public Health Policy

In addition to the important role of education policy in the creation of recovery high schools, public health policy is also critical to their functioning due to the mental and physical health implications of adolescent SUDs. If public health departments recognize that adolescent addiction is a health issue and not simply a behavioral problem (Fisher & Harrison, 2012), then they can work to provide appropriate SUD treatment and mental health supports.

Because most schools rely on referrals from treatment providers for a large percentage of their students, states that have a higher percentage of adolescents receiving treatment for SUDs may be in a better position to open recovery schools due to the higher number of identifiable applicants. Several statewide policies likely contribute to Minnesota's relatively high number of adolescents receiving SUD treatment. Beginning in July 2008, all counties, tribes, and Managed Care Organizations were required under Rule 25 to provide assessments for chemical use to anyone who requested one (Minnesota Department of Human Services, 2014). Individuals who meet (1) clinical requirements for addiction and (2) specified financial requirements (relative to the poverty line) are eligible to have their treatment costs covered by the Consolidated Chemical Dependency Treatment Fund (CCDTF), a fund established in 1986 to pool state and federal treatment funds. The CCDTF covers the most cost-effective program and level of care available for individuals without insurance or for those who have already used the maximum amount of funding allocated by their insurer (Minnesota Department of Human Services, 2014). All licensed treatment providers are eligible to receive CCDTF funds and must compete with other providers as they negotiate prices with the counties. A reserve fund also exists in case a county exhausts all of its available resources (Minnesota Statutes, Chapter 254B). Three recovery schools in Moberg and Finch's (2007) study cited the presence of Rule 25 and the associated CCDTF as positively impacting their enrollment.

Additionally, in response to the 2002 Minnesota Department of Human Services task force's recommendation to improve the state's mental health system, in 2003 the Minnesota Legislature passed a law requiring mental health screening for juvenile justice populations (Statute 260B.157). The legislature recognized that a large percentage of adolescents had mental health or co-occurring disorders, including SUDs. This statute along with the Rule 25 and the CCDTF have likely contributed to the relatively high percentage of adolescents receiving treatment in Minnesota.

Results of Fertilized Grassroots Advocacy

Following the education and public health policy foundation in Minnesota, the first two recovery high schools opened there in the late 1980s: Sobriety High (1987) and PEASE Academy (1989). Education policies provided the structure to open recovery high schools, but as their histories illustrate, these schools emerged in the presence of dedicated individuals who perceived the need, understood the nature of adolescent recovery, and had the resources needed to help spark the creation of a recovery school. We refer to these efforts as "fertilized grassroots advocacy" because the policy context was ripe for such efforts to take root, but the local advocacy efforts were needed to plant and cultivate recovery schools within that fertile environment.

School Origins. We can trace the origin of the first two Minnesota schools, Sobriety High and PEASE Academy, to Carol Robson, who started the New Dimensions School, a private, non-profit school in St. Louis Park, Minnesota, in 1981. The school was designed for students in grades 1-12 who had exceptional needs, and Robson started the school to provide a more appropriate setting for her elementary-aged son, who had speech and writing challenges.

Based in part on suggestions from the school's teacher, Bruce McLean, and collaboration with Robson's friend, Ralph Neiditch, who worked at the Hazelden alcohol and drug treatment facility in Minnesota, New Dimensions started enrolling students who had received treatment for a SUD (McLean personal communication, March 4, 2016). By 1987, New Dimensions had become a program for adolescent students in grades nine through 12 who had completed an alcohol/chemical or emotional/behavior treatment regimen (Williams, 1987). In the beginning, students with SUDs were simply part of the overall student body, but as Robson's son, who did not have a substance use disorder, completed his time at the school in 1988, the school transitioned into exclusively enrolling students who had received treatment for SUD. In April 1988, the school changed its name to "Ecole Nouvelle" ("New School"), and in July 1988, based on students' recommendations, the school became "Sobriety High."

In addition to the school, Carol Robson and her husband, Sheridan, had run the Summit House in St. Louis Park, Minnesota, since 1976. Summit House was a group home for young people ages 9-25 who had cognitive, emotional, and behavioral disabilities. Two men who worked for Summit House were Ken Simon, a graduate student teacher who worked as a weekend staff member, and Joe Mailman, son of a wealthy Northeastern family who was in recovery. Mailman had worked at Hazelden, where he met Carol Robson, and she hired him to work at Summit House. Robson invited Simon to visit New Dimensions soon after it had transitioned into a recovery high school during the 1987-1988 school year (Robson personal communication, April 22, 2016).

Simon observed McLean teaching and was impressed by the concept. He mentioned it to Mailman and to a fellow teacher at Osseo Middle School, Barbara Schmidt (Simon personal communication, January 9, 2016). Schmidt had a background in pastoral counseling and juvenile court case management. The three of them were so inspired by the idea of providing a safe, sober school as a "transition point for students until their sobriety was strong enough to be able to return to their regular school" that they formed a non-profit called "the Holos Foundation Inc. Transition School for Recovering Chemically Dependent Youth" in June 1988 (Department of the Treasury, 1988, p. 2). Schmidt came up with the name "Holos" to represent the holistic consciousness element of life. The organization's mission was "expanding personal capacities and potentials through the development of body, mind, and spirit," and those principles were essential to the non-traditional curriculum they created for the school (Fluor, personal communication, May 3, 2016).

On January 30, 1989, the Holos school had its first day of classes in a Minneapolis community building with a handful of students. The school had two main goals. First, the school intended "to help recovering youth make a positive, healthy (chemical free) transition back into the public school system." Second, the school would "help recovering youth develop skills which will assist them in succeeding academically with the public school." (Department of the Treasury, 1988, p. 2).

Although the initial goal of Holos was to keep students enrolled for only a few months, the staff realized that students preferred not to return to their traditional schools, and thus the purpose changed by fall 1989 to keeping students as long as they wanted to stay, up to and including graduation. Enrollment reached 12 by the end of the semester, by which time the students had renamed the school "Imagination Peers Enjoying A Sober Education (PEASE) Academy." Schmidt felt that was too long, thus they decided to drop the name "Imagination," and "PEASE Academy" was born (Fluor personal communication, May 5, 2016).

State Policies. Although Sobriety High and PEASE Academy emerged from grassroots efforts, those grassroots were "fertilized" by state policies. New Dimensions (which became Sobriety High) began as a private school, charging about $150/month tuition, but it also received funds available for organizations serving youth identified as at-risk (Robson personal communication, April 22, 2016). In time, Sobriety High became a "contract alternative school," establishing a contract with the Edina school district. Holos (which became PEASE Academy) opened as a "contract alternative school" through a contract with Minneapolis Public Schools (Fluor personal communication, May 4, 2016).

Holos/PEASE also utilized the High School Graduation Incentives (HSGI) program, which had become law in 1987, to offer valid credits. In its IRS documents (Department of the Treasury, 1988, p. 2), Holos Foundation stated, "Credits will be awarded by the Minneapolis Public Schools for Minneapolis district residents and non-district residents who qualify to register in Minneapolis under the Minnesota Graduation High School Incentives Act of 1987 (all youth diagnosed as chemically dependent qualify)."

Both schools pre-dated the landmark Charter School legislation of 1991. In time, though, this law would allow the schools to establish solid financial ground and generate robust enrollments. This is another example of how grassroots programs ultimately benefited from public policies that may or may not have been in existence when the programs began.

School Growth/Demise. Over time, the staffing and structure of both schools evolved. After Carol Robson's son transitioned out of New Dimensions/Sobriety High, she too soon moved on from the school. A formal board was created, and Ralph Neidtich took on the primary leadership role. He negotiated with a local suburban school district to relocate Sobriety High to Edina, Minnesota, in 1991. Sobriety High continued to grow and flourish, opening school campuses at multiple locations over the years. However, in 2013, all Sobriety High campuses closed due to lack of funding (National Authorizer – Charter School Catalog website, 2013).

PEASE Academy remains open today as the oldest existing recovery high school, though the founders were only part of the school during its first few years. The school moved to its permanent location in a Lutheran church near the campus of the University of Minnesota in the summer of 1990. It is now part of a larger charter school organization – the Minnesota Transitions Charter Schools (MTCS). Although many factors have likely influenced PEASE's sustainability, discussions with school staff and site visits suggest that primary factors include charter school funding, their central urban location, a large student population (typically 60-75 students), and the capacity to take in new students as other schools close.

Community Factors

The efforts of passionate individuals (those described here and others) bore fruit in Minnesota; based on our data collection, from 1987-2006, 23 recovery high schools operated in the state of Minnesota, which is almost four times the number of schools that have *ever* operated in any other single state. Unfortunately, since 2006, the number of schools in operation has declined from 13 to only four left in operation in 2016. The decline in recovery schools in Minnesota brings us to our final component for review: community factors interacting with top-down policies and grassroots advocacy that may influence the sustainability of recovery schools.

Access Challenges. Although the open enrollment legislation, Rule 25, and the CCDTF, appear to have contributed to the development of recovery high schools in Minnesota, many interested students have not been referred to the schools or have been unable to attend because of a lack of transportation. A survey conducted by the Minnesota Recovery Schools Task Force (2009) found that although 93% of recovery school referral sources felt that recovery high schools would be beneficial to their clients, 40% felt that transportation was a primary barrier to attendance. Moberg and Finch (2007) also noted that one school serving students from a wide geographic area reported that most of their students came from outside the district, and described the lack of transportation as one of the main reasons they were unable to reach their desired capacity for financial viability (30-35 students). For the first several years of this school's operation, other districts transported their students to the school, but when districts stopped providing transportation, enrollment at the school dropped to less than 25 students.

Transportation is clearly a major obstacle for most recovery schools, although it was not cited as an issue by the only recovery school that is located in an urban area convenient to various public transportation lines. For other

begins from a backward mapping framework and discussing the grassroots advocacy that occurred there.

School Origins. In 2004, William Ostiguy, then head of the employee assistance program at the Boston firefighters' union, was researching programs to help the families of firefighters whose children had drug or alcohol issues (personal communication, school principal, January 12, 2013). Sobriety High had received national publicity in the late 1990s and early 2000s, and Ostiguy contacted Sobriety High's director, Judi Hanson, for information about recovery high schools. The director connected him with a Sobriety High student whose family lived in Massachusetts (Hanson personal communication, April 16, 2006). At the time, the student was a junior at the Sobriety High campus in Edina, and when she returned home to Massachusetts for summer break, Ostiguy set up a meeting with this student, a former mayor of Boston (Thomas Menino), a former State Senator (Steven Tolman), the former chairperson of the Interagency Council on Substance Abuse, and the executive director of the Gavin Foundation. The student graduated from Sobriety High in 2005 and made starting a recovery high school a priority when she returned home after commencement. The state government created a five-year grant in 2006 for three recovery high schools, which opened in October 2006. Using these influential connections, this team then advocated for recovery high schools as a public health program in need of state funding and support.

In Massachusetts, recovery high schools were thus initiated by the efforts of advocates who leveraged support by drawing on their connections with people in positions of power to successfully establish a state-level funding mechanism. A call for proposals was announced and individuals submitted requests for funding to open schools (personal communication, school principal, May 2013). Three recovery schools were subsequently opened in 2006 and were initially funded through a five-year grant from the Department of Public Health. A fourth recovery school opened through a similar grant in 2012 (Mass.gov, 2012), and another opened in 2015. The five-year grants were renewed in 2011, maintaining the schools' primary funding through the Department of Public Health. We will now consider the specific public health and education policies that were instrumental in the establishment and funding of Massachusetts' recovery high schools.

Public Health Policy. Massachusetts integrates substance abuse prevention and treatment into primary medical care (Botticelli, 2013). As a result, statewide healthcare legislation that provides for mental health services has established a system of treatment and recovery support for adolescents.

For example, Massachusetts was the first state to provide Medicaid managed care for mental health and substance abuse care, which substantially expanded access to such care (Dickey, Normand, Norton, Rupp, & Azeni, 2001). Another source of public health funding afforded to recovery high schools comes through health insurance. For example, the Boston recovery school employs a licensed substance abuse counselor who is paid out of Department of Public Health funding. Through the Gavin Foundation, two counselors also provide services at the school once a week. Because the Foundation can provide counseling through their outpatient license, insurance companies often agree to cover the services.

In addition to the increased access to SUD treatment, state policies also dictate certain eligibility requirements recovery high schools must meet in order to qualify for the Department of Public Health funding. Massachusetts defines the term "Recovery High School" as "a public school or collaborative program for students diagnosed with substance use disorder or dependency, as defined by the Diagnostic and Statistical Manual of Mental Disorders IV-TR" (Chapter 71, Section 91). The schools provide comprehensive education and recovery services; thus, they are viewed as a product and responsibility of the education and public health sectors, and these departments have the authority to "promulgate rules and regulations, as necessary" (Chapter 71, Section 91). Recovery schools are required to send student data to the Massachusetts Department of Public Health (Chapter 71), and each school principal works with the Department of Public Health to ensure complete reporting.

Although this multi-system collaboration makes the recovery high schools possible, it also presents challenges. For example, in the near future, new administrative procedures will impact the schools' organization and planning. Chapter 257, legislation that recently changed to apply to all Massachusetts human-service programs, requires a system of accountability for the funding stream of all such programs. Specifically, instead of receiving an initial payment of $500,000 annually from the Department of Public Health, under Chapter 257 the funding system will change to a cost-reimbursement payment plan. This means that schools will need to submit a request for payment based on actual student enrollment, requiring more of each school's limited administrative resources. Additionally, with the reimbursement system in place under the $500,000 grant, the schools do not have the option to receive funding greater than the already allotted grant if enrollment need outweighs the funding. In other words, this administrative change in funding procedures will not result in more funding for the schools, but instead will result in more administrative work required to receive the same amount of money.

Education Policy. Massachusetts state legislation also provides financial support for recovery high schools through the education sector. Chapter 70 education aid legislation is used to determine and distribute appropriate funding to Massachusetts public schools; this legislation ensures that schools have enough resources to provide for their students while taking into account what their local funding can contribute (Massachusetts Budget and Policy Center, February 2014). Section 91 of Chapter 71 mandates that recovery high schools must be provided with an annual student allocation that matches the Chapter 70 per student allotment. If the only recovery high school option is outside the student's school district, and the student chooses to attend that school, their school district must pay the recovery high school the "state average foundation budget." When the student completes state and district graduation requirements, the district and recovery high school together confer the student's diploma. In return, recovery high schools must submit whatever data the board considers necessary to track students' academic progress and outcomes.

Although recovery schools are expected to communicate education data, coordination between the school district and recovery high schools in Massachusetts has not always been straightforward. One reason for this lack of clarity might be the geographic dispersion of the five schools across the state (Beverly, Boston, Brockton, Springfield, and Worcester). In recent years, a concerted effort has been made to institute stronger regulations and reporting mechanisms while still allowing each unique recovery school the flexibility to craft their own identities. Even with these regulations, recovery high schools can differ to the point that their student populations and day-to-day operations look markedly different (Schwartzapfel, 2011). One recovery high school principal (personal communication, May 2013) described this dynamic, stating: "schools develop their own kind of brand… a lot depends on the structure of the schools and where they reside in their district, who do they respond to, how much autonomy they have."

Community Factors

The expansion of recovery high schools in Massachusetts brings us to our final component: community level factors currently interacting with the top-down policies and local advocacy efforts that may influence the future of recovery high schools in Massachusetts.

Referral Challenges. The integration of Massachusetts's recovery high schools with the public school system conveys certain advantages, including increased funding opportunities, but this relationship also brings an overwhelming amount of administrative detail for the daily operation of the schools and the ongoing student referral process between schools. Although the recovery school has a standard intake policy including specific eligibility requirements, the school's use of multiple referral sources poses some challenges. One critical aspect is ensuring that all referral sources are knowledgeable about the intake process and admission criteria. For example, some recovery schools have strict guidelines requiring students to complete some form of SUD treatment before enrolling at the school. Thus, for school staff invested in the success of their students, deciding what to do with referred students who are not in recovery, such as those who may still be using substances and are not committed to sobriety, is a major challenge.

Access Challenges. In addition to referral challenges, recovery high schools also have to make tough choices about who to admit. Because students who are referred from other schools who have not had – or do not want to have – formal treatment sometimes do not meet the admission criteria, they cannot attend the recovery school and will have to find an alternative schooling option or be routed to the juvenile justice system. Although recovery high schools adhere to their admission criteria to ensure a safe and effective recovery community, this process also illustrates how inequity can be perpetuated (Oser, Karakos, & Hennessy, 2016). Currently in Massachusetts, a student identified in a substance-related violation by a school or law enforcement official can have two different possible consequences. The youth can be suspended or expelled from school; or, the student can be arrested and brought to a court hearing. The court can then send the youth to the juvenile justice system *or* to the adult criminal justice system. In this situation, youth whose families have the financial resources and supports required for SUD treatment can often avoid drug-related sentences. However, data indicate that certain minority populations in the Boston area often receive less SUD treatment than others (Boston Public Health Commission Research Office, 2010). Thus, when students are referred to the recovery school but denied admission because they have not received treatment, disparities in access are created. Without proper and timely intervention, substance use continues and a substance-related offense is more likely to occur.

One project, *Changing Tracks*, has been initiated to provide services in Boston to youth in high-need neighborhoods identified by Boston's Juvenile Court (Action for Boston Community Development, Inc., 2013; Oser,

Karakos, & Hennessy, 2016). Changing Tracks will address this issue through a multi-pronged approach including building stakeholder alliances and treatment awareness in schools and communities; creating a school-based referral system; creating a city-wide court diversion system; improving treatment by including wrap-around supports (such as recovery high schools) and by incorporating culturally-appropriate treatments. This initiative is made possible by funding from a private foundation and schools' collaboration with Boston's Juvenile Court.

Discussion

Similar to Minnesota, a spark in Massachusetts ignited the formation of grassroots coalitions. In Minnesota the initial catalyst involved the existence of alternative school and school choice policies, but in Massachusetts, passionate individuals advocated for state legislation specific to recovery high schools that became the driving force in founding the four recovery high schools. Using backward mapping, we see how passionate individuals, a recovery school student and a firefighter, were integral in advocating politically connected individuals for legislation to create recovery high schools. Consequently, state-level policies were created; from this point, forward mapping highlights how the schools were products of governmental competitive funding and thus follow certain administrative processes. Agencies at many levels – from the state to local foundations – have a stake in the implementation and operation of recovery high schools in Massachusetts. As a result, the schools have both local and state-level champions.

Currently, the recovery high schools in Massachusetts are more stable than the recovery high schools in Minnesota; no schools have closed, and no schools have openly discussed this possibility. This apparent stability likely stems in part from the relatively recent establishment of these schools, but is more likely mainly due to the secure funding from the Department of Public Health. This sense of financial security has allowed school staff to spend time envisioning broader changes in adolescent recovery supports, such as the *Changing Tracks* program. The case of Massachusetts thus highlights the ways that a slightly different trajectory, of initial grassroots efforts leading to specific policy-level changes, has led to a seemingly more sustainable school model that also continues to grapple with the challenges of working at the intersection of education, public health, and juvenile justice sectors.

CONCLUSION

The history and current status of recovery high schools in both states highlights the diverse forces that have given rise to recovery high schools. The social ecological model of public health behavior helps us understand these similar yet importantly different cases by highlighting the reciprocal influences between individuals, contexts, and public health programming (Sallis et al., 2008). For those in Minnesota, the policy context created a fertile environment for recovery high schools, to which individuals responded with efforts to create each school. In Massachusetts, individuals advocated for and achieved policy changes specific to recovery schools. It is in the midst of these evolving interactions within the ecological context that people and organizations must function. The history and future prospects of recovery high schools in Minnesota and Massachusetts highlight the complexities in each state, revealing the interaction of proximal and distal forces in the course of this community-based continuing care support. Both cases demonstrate the need for some degree of advocacy and local support in conjunction with a facilitative policy context; however, they also illustrate what happens when the trajectories of development diverge. In Minnesota, the proliferation of recovery high schools, although exceptional, was not met by equally rapid and program-specific changes in policy, and the burgeoning schools eventually declined to a much smaller number of recovery schools. In Massachusetts, initial advocacy efforts generated policy-level changes that led to the creation of the schools, allowing the development of policy and schools to happen such that neither force outpaced the growth of the other. As one Massachusetts recovery school principal asserted: "You have to have your champions and advocates in your communities who have access to, I hate to say this, to power, to decision makers, otherwise the schools that try to do it by raising private money, that's not going to work..." (personal communication, May 2013).

The recent establishment of a Recovery Branch within the federal Office of National Drug Control Policy (ONDCP) illustrates an increasing federal government commitment to support people in recovery. Communities clearly play a critical role in this process, and the cases of Minnesota and Massachusetts demonstrate the multiple grassroots and policy-level forces that influence recovery high schools. Models of community empowerment can be particularly relevant in helping communities hoping to open a recovery high school or similar youth-serving program understand how to facilitate collaborative partnerships with multiple stakeholders (Fawcett et al., 1995). It is thus critical to generate both grassroots and policy-level support, recognizing and drawing on the available sources of power in each community (Pentz, 2000). One provision of the Affordable Care Act is designed to increase the mental health resources available to communities, so it is crucial to continue to explore how school, district, county, state, and national forces facilitate or hinder the provision of these resources. We have seen in these cases that a combination of policies to provide resources and structure, in combination with local advocates, is essential to recovery high schools' success. We must as communities, therefore, continue to balance the call for individual efforts with an appeal to our governing bodies to provide the supports adolescents need as they work toward long-term recovery.

REFERENCES

Action for Boston Community Development, Inc. (2013). William J. Ostiguy recovery high school annual report: School year 2012-2013. Retrieved from http://ostiguyhigh.org/wp-content/uploads/2012/11/ June_11_WEB. pdf (Archived by WebCite® at http://www.webcitation.org/6Vs8CDwU6).

Allison, K. W., Crawford, I., Leone, P. E., Trickett, E., Perez-Febles, A., Burton, L. M. & Le Blanc, R. (1999). Adolescent substance use: Preliminary examinations of school and neighborhood context. *American Journal of Community Psychology*, *27*(2), 111-141.

Association of Recovery Schools. (2014, February). ARS member recovery high schools. Retrieved from http://www.recoveryschools.org/schools.

Association of Recovery Schools. (2016). The State of Recovery High Schools, 2016 Biennial Report. Denton, TX. Retrieved from www.recoveryschools.org.

Boston Public Health Commission Research Office. (2010). Health of Boston [Chapter 13: Substance Abuse]. Boston, MA: Boston Public Health Commission. Retrieved from http://www.bphc.org/about/research/hob2010/Pages/Home.aspx.

Botticelli, M. (2013, January 25). Commentary: The public health approach to a balanced drug policy. Retrieved from http://www.drugfree.org/join-together/drugs/commentary-the-public-health-approach-to-a-balanced-drug-policy.

Boyd, W. L., Hare, D. & Nathan, J. (2002). What really happened? Minnesota's experience with statewide public school choice programs.

Retrieved from http://www.texastech.edu/news/ CurrentNews/display_article.php?id=2081.

Bronfenbrenner, U. (1979). The ecology of human development: Experiments by nature and design. Boston: Harvard University Press.

Burleson, J. A., Kaminer, Y. & Burke, R. H. (2012). Twelve-month follow-up of aftercare for adolescents with alcohol use disorders. *Journal of Substance Abuse Treatment*, *42*, 78-86.

Department of the Treasury, Internal Revenue Service, (1988, June). Form 1023: Application for Recognition of Exemption.

Dickey, B., Normand, S. L., Norton, E. C., Rupp, A. & Azeni, H. (2001). Managed care and children's behavioral health services in Massachusetts. *Psychiatric Services*, *52*, 183-188.

Doyle, P. (2001, April 29). School aid bill blasted as biased; It appears Sobriety High would be the lone beneficiary under a $1.3 million plan for alternative schools. *Minneapolis Star-Tribune*. Accessed online: https://www.highbeam.com/doc/1G1-73859641.html/.

Elmore, (1979). Backward mapping: Implementation research and policy decisions. *Political Science Quarterly*, *94*, 601-616.

Erikson, E. (1968). Identity: Youth and crisis. Oxford, England: Norton & Co.

Farris-Berg, K. & Schroeder, J. (2003). Alternative-education programs: The quiet giant in Minnesota public education. *Education Evolving*. A report by the Center for Policy Studies and Hamline University.

Fawcett, S. B., Paine-Andrews, A., Francisco, V. T., Schultz, J. A., Richter, K. P., Lewis, R. K. & Williams, E. L. (1995). Using empowerment theory in collaborative partnerships for community health and development. *American Journal of Community Psychology*, *23*(5), 677-697.

Finch, A. J., Moberg, D. P. & Krupp, A. L. (2014). Continuing care in high schools: A descriptive study of recovery high school programs. *Journal of Child and Adolescent Substance Abuse*, *23*(2), 116-129.

Finch, A. J., Moberg, P. D., Tanner-Smith, E. & Karakos, H. L. (2014, April). Recovery High Schools: Innovative Schools Supporting Recovery From Substance Abuse. Paper presented at the meeting of the American Educational Research Association, Philadelphia, PA.

Fisher, E. A. (2014). Recovery supports for young people: What do existing supports reveal about the recovery environment? *Peabody Journal of Education*, *89*(2), 258-270.

Fisher, G. L. & Harrison, T. C. (2012). Substance abuse: Information for school counselors, social workers, therapists, and counselors (5th ed.). Upper Saddle River, NJ: Pearson.

Gessner, J. (2013, June 3). Sobriety High School closing its doors June 7. *ABC Newspapers*. Retrieved from http:// abcnewspapers.com/ 2013/06/03/ sobriety-high-school-closing-its-doors-june-7/.

Jones, D. J., Heflinger, C. A. & Saunders, R. C. (2007). The ecology of adolescent substance abuse service utilization. *American Journal of Community Psychology*, *40*(3-4), 345-358.

Karakos, H. L. (2014). Positive peer support or negative peer influence? The role of peers among adolescents in recovery high schools. *Peabody Journal of Education*, *89*(2), 214-228.

Kelly, J. F. & Urbanoski, K. (2012). Youth recovery contexts: The incremental effects of 12 step attendance and involvement on adolescent outpatient outcomes. *Alcoholism: Clinical and Experimental Research*, *36*, 1219-1229.

Kochanek, T. T. (2008). Recovery high schools in Massachusetts: A promising, comprehensive model for adolescent substance abuse and dependence. Retrieved from http://massrecoveryhs.org/documents/ RecoveryHighSchooloverview.pdf.

Laws of Minnesota 1991 chapter 265, article 9, section 3 (2014, April 10). Retrieved from https://www.revisor.mn.gov/laws/?id=265&year=1991& type=0.

Lewin, K. (1951). *Field theory in the social sciences.* New York: Harper.

Mass.gov. (2012, January 19). Lieutenant Governor Murray celebrates grand opening of Commonwealth's 4th recovery school. Retrieved from http:// www.mass.gov/governor/pressoffice/pressreleases/2012/2012119-opening -of-independence-academy-brockton.html.

Massachusetts Budget and Policy Center, (2014, February 15). Demystifying the Chapter 70 formula: How the Massachusetts education funding system works. Retrieved from http://www.massbudget.org/report_window.php? loc=Facts_10_22_10.html.

Minnesota Department of Human Services, (2014, April 10). Disabilities: Alcohol and drug abuse: Laws and rules. Retrieved from http://www .dhs.state.mn.us/disabilities.

Minnesota Recovery Schools Task Force, (2009). Minnesota Recovery Schools Task Force legislative platform. Minneapolis, MN: Monique Bourgeois, Traci Bowermaster, & Heidi Judge.

Minnesota State Legislature, (2014a). HF 2326, 88th Legislature (2013-2014). Retrieved from https://www.revisor.mn.gov/bills/bill.php?f=HF2326 &b= house&y=2014&ssn=0.

Minnesota State Legislature, (2014b). SF 1925. 88th Legislature (2013-2014). Retrieved from https://www.revisor.mn.gov/bills/bill.php?f=SF1925 &b= senate&y=2014&ssn=0.

Minnesota Statutes, Chapter 254B, Chemical Dependency Treatment (2014, April 10). Retrieved from https://www.revisor.mn.gov/statutes/?id=254B.

Moberg, D. P. & Finch, A. J. (2007). Recovery high schools: A descriptive study of school programs and students. *Journal of Groups in Addiction and Recovery*, *2* (2-4), 128-161.

Moberg, D. P., Finch, A. J., Winters, K. C. & Lipsey, M. W. (2013, May). Preventing academic failure and substance use relapse through recovery high schools. Poster session presented at the meeting of the Society for Prevention Research, Washington, DC.

Moberg, D. P., Finch, A. J. & Lindsley, S M. (2014). Recovery high schools: Students and responsive academic and therapeutic services. *Peabody Journal of Education*, *89*(2), 165-182.

National Authorizer – Charter School Catalog, (2013, September). Sobriety High- Alliance Academy Burnsville. Retrieved from http://catalog. charterschoolcenter.org/school/sobriety-high-alliance-academy-burnsville.

National Institute on Drug Abuse, (2014, January). Principles of adolescent substance use disorder treatment: A research-based guide. Retrieved from http://www.drugabuse.gov/sites/default/files/podata_1_17_14.pdf.

Office of National Drug Control Policy, (2014). *National drug control strategy*. Washington, D.C.: Office of National Drug Control Policy. Retrieved from http://www.whitehouse.gov/sites/default/files/ ondcp/policy-and-research/ndcs_2014.pdf.

Oser, R., Karakos, H. & Hennessy, E. A. (2016). Disparities in youth access to substance abuse treatment and recovery services: How one recovery school initiative is helping students "Change Tracks." Unpublished manuscript.

Pentz, M. A. (2000). Institutionalizing community-based prevention through policy change. *Journal of Community Psychology*, *28*(3), 257-270.

Sallis, J. F., Owen, N. & Fisher, E. B. (2008). Ecological models of health behavior. In *Health behavior and health education: Theory, research, and practice*, (Vol. *4*, pp. 465-486). Jossey-Bass San Francisco, CA.

Schwartzapfel, Beth (2011, November). Reading, writing, and rehab. *Boston Magazine*, Retrieved from http:// www.bostonmagazine.com/ 2011/10/ reading-writing-and-rehab/.

Substance Abuse and Mental Health Services Administration, (2012). Center for Behavioral Health Statistics and Quality, Substance Abuse and Mental

- Finch, A.J. and Karakos, H. (2014). Substance abuse recovery and schooling: The role of recovery high schools and collegiate recovery communities. *Peabody Journal of Education, 89*(2), 159-164.
- Finch, A.J. and Frieden, G. (2014). The ecological and developmental role of recovery schools. *Peabody Journal of Education, 89*(2), 271-287.
- Moberg, D.P, Finch, A.J., and Lindsley, S. (2014). Recovery high schools: Students and responsive academic and therapeutic services. *Peabody Journal of Education, 89*(2), 165-182.
- DePue, K., Finch, A.J., and Nation, M. (2014). The bottoming out experience and the turning point: A phenomenology of the cognitive shift from drinker to non-drinker. *Journal of Addictions and Offender Counseling, 35*(1), 38-56.

Book Chapters

- Finch, A.J., Oluchi Nwosu, Gina Frieden, Craig Anne Heflinger, Allison McGuire, Sarah V. Suiter, Emily Hennessey, Emily Burchfield, Nina C. Martin, Linda Isaacs, Lauren Brinkley-Rubenstein, Paul Speer, Abbey Mann, Sharon Shields, Neal Palmer, Bethany Pittman, and Sandra Barnes. (In Press). "Can Synergy Across Theory, Pedagogy, and Practice Guide Professional Education? The Community Development and Action (CDA) and Human Development and Counseling (HDC) Graduate Experiences" by In Barnes, S. (Ed.) *Academics in Action.*

Other Journal Articles & Scholarly Work

- Finch, A.J. (Jan/Feb 2015). Why do we need recovery high schools? *Counselor Magazine.*

Name: Emily A. Hennessy
Affiliation: Vanderbilt University, Peabody College
Education: PhD candidate, Community Research and Action, Vanderbilt University
M.Phil., Health Promotion, University of Bergen, Norway
BA, Psychology, Gordon College, Wenham, MA USA
Address: 230 Appleton Place, PMB #90 Nashville, TN 37203

Honors:

- Recipient, James N Morgan Fund for New Directions in the Analysis of Complex Interactions (2015)
- Fulbright Scholar, University of Bergen, Norway (2008–2009)

Publications Last 3 Years:

- **Hennessy, E. A.**, Tanner-Smith, E. E., & Steinka-Fry, K. T. (2015). Do brief alcohol interventions reduce tobacco use among youth? A systematic review and meta-analysis. *Journal of Behavioral Medicine, 38*(6), 899-911. doi:10.1007/s10865-015-9653-2
- Fisher, B. W., & **Hennessy, E. A.** The relationship between school resource officers and school-based disciplinary incidents: A Meta-analysis. *Adolescent Research Review*, in press.
- Polanin, J. R., Tanner-Smith, E. E., **Hennessy, E. A.** (2015). Estimating the difference between published and unpublished effect sizes: A meta-review. *Reviews of Educational Research*, epub. doi:10.3102/0034654315582067
- Steinka-Fry, K. T., Tanner-Smith, E. E., & **Hennessy, E. A.** (2015). Effects of brief alcohol interventions on drinking and driving among underage youth: A systematic review and meta-analysis. *Journal of Addiction and Prevention, 3*, 11.
- Tanner-Smith, E., Steinka-Fry, K. T., **Hennessy, E. A.**, Lipsey, M.W., & Winters, K. C. (2015). Secondary effects of brief alcohol interventions on substance use among youth: A systematic review and meta-analysis. *Journal of Youth and Adolescence, 44*, 1011-1023. doi:10.1007/s10964-015-0252-x
- **Hennessy, E. A.,** & Fisher, B. W. (2015). A meta-analysis exploring the relationship between 12-Step attendance and adolescent substance use relapse. *Journal of Groups in Addiction and Recovery, 10*, 79-96. http://dx.doi.org/10.1080/1556035X.2015.999621
- **Hennessy, E. A.** & Tanner-Smith E. (2014). Effectiveness of brief school-based alcohol interventions: A systematic review and meta-analysis. *Prevention Science, 16*(3), 463-474. doi:10.1007/s11121-014-0512-0
- **Fisher, E. A.** (2014). Recovery supports for young people: What do existing supports reveal about the recovery environment? *Peabody Journal of Education, 89*(2): 258-270.

Name: Holly L. Karakos
Affiliation: Equal Opportunity Schools
Education: Ph.D., Community Research and Action, Vanderbilt University
MA, Psychology, Wake Forest University
BA, Psychology, Religion, Furman University
Address: 7344 NE 192nd St., Kenmore, WA 98028

Research and Professional Experience: I have been studying youth development and education in a number of contexts for 8 years, including recovery high schools, youth civic engagement, and research and practice in educational equity.

Professional Appointments: Currently, Research Analyst at Equal Opportunity Schools.

Publications Last 3 Years:

- Karakos, H. L., Voight, A. M., Geller, J. G., Nation, M., & Nixon, C. (in press). Student civic participation and school climate: Associations at multiple levels of the school ecology. *Journal of Community Psychology*.
- Karakos, H. L., & Wray-Lake, L. (2014). Sociopolitical development and positive youth development: Emerging themes from the 2014 youth civic engagement preconference from the Biennial Meeting of the Society for Research on Adolescence. *International Journal of Developmental Science*, *8*(3-4), 155-158.
- Karakos, H. L. (2014). Positive peer support or negative peer influence? The role of peers among adolescents in recovery high schools. *Peabody Journal of Education*, *89*(2), 214-228.
- Finch, A. J., & Karakos, H. L. (2014). Substance abuse recovery and schooling: The role of recovery high schools and collegiate recovery communities [special issue]. *Peabody Journal of Education*, *89*(2), 159-164.
- Geller, J. G., Voight, A. M., Wegman, H. L., & Nation, M. (2013). How do varying types of youth civic engagement relate to perceptions of school climate? *Applied Developmental Science*, *17(3)*, 135-147.
- Karakos, H. L., Fisher, B., Geller, J., Lunn, L., Palmer, N., Perkins, D., Mihaylov, N., Partridge, W., & Shields, S. (2015). The field school in intercultural education as a model for international service-learning and collaborative action research training. In S. L. Barnes (Ed.) *Academics in Action!* Bronx, NY: Fordham University Press.

INDEX

A

T

U

V

W

Y